Antigua
& Barbuda
DIRECTIONS

REDCLIFFE STREET

WRITTEN AND RESEARCHED BY

Adam Vaitilingam

THIS EDITION UPDATED AND RESEARCHED BY

Christopher P. Hamilton

ROUGH GUIDES

NEW YORK • LONDON • DELHI

www.roughguides.com

Contents

Introduction 4

Ideas 9

The big six 10
Beaches 12
Restaurants 14
Colonial forts 16
On the water 18
Antiguan specialities 20
Museums and galleries 22
Hikes 24
Entertainment and nightlife 26
Great views 28
Barbuda 30

Places 33

St John's 35
The northwest coast 51
The Atlantic coast 60

Falmouth and English Harbour 71
The west coast 90
Barbuda and Redonda 101

Essentials 111

Arrival 113
Island transport 113
Information and maps 115
Money and costs 116
Communications and the media 117
Accommodation 118
Food and drink 119
Ocean and beach safety 120
Sport and outdoor activities 121
Crime and personal safety 127
Travelling with children 127
Festivals and events 128
Directory 129

Index 137

Introduction to

Antigua
& Barbuda

Little known just a generation ago, tiny Antigua has established itself as one of the Caribbean's more popular destinations. The island is dotted with superb white-sand beaches, many of which – despite the upswing in tourism that has given birth to dozens of excellent restaurants and hotels, and a handful of all-inclusives – remain relatively uncrowded. If you're looking to crash on a stretch of sand for a week or two, you'll find this laid-back, welcoming isle hard to beat.

◄ Breadfruit

Some of the best beaches are at Dickenson Bay in the northwest, Half Moon Bay in the east and Rendezvous Bay in the south. Of these, only Dickenson Bay forms part of a major tourist strip; the others – as well as several more just like them – are much less built up than similarly idyllic spots in the Caribbean. The waters surrounding Antigua are also a prime spot for spray-soaked watersports, with excellent scuba diving and snorkelling opportunities in the fabulous offshore reefs.

Before Europeans began colonizing the West Indies, Antigua was populated by Arawak-speaking Amerindians. Sighted by Columbus in 1493, the island was left to its own devices until the early sixteenth century, when British settlers arrived, bringing with them

When to visit

For many visitors, Antigua's leading attraction is its **tropical climate:** hot and sunny all year round. The weather is at its best from mid-December to mid-April, with rainfall low and the heat tempered by cooling trade winds. Things can get noticeably hotter during the summer and, particularly in September and October, the humidity can become oppressive. September is also the most threatening month of the annual hurricane season, which runs officially from June 1 to October 31.

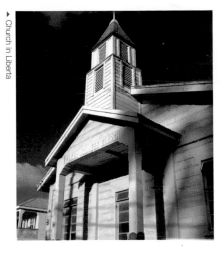

◄ Church in Liberta

African slaves to clear the native vegetation and plant sugarcane. For centuries, the island was little more than a giant sugar factory, producing sugar and rum to send home to an increasingly sweet-toothed mother country. Around Antigua, the tall brick foundations of a hundred deserted and decaying sugar mills, as well as the ruins of military forts and signal stations, bear witness to that long colonial era.

These relics make for worthy diversions if you can drag yourself away from your patch of sand. The superbly restored naval dockyard and the crumbling forts around English Harbour and Shirley Heights are as impressive as any historic site in the West Indies. There

◄ Runaway Bay

▲ Antiguan steel band

◄ Shirley Heights

are lots of other little nuggets to explore too, including the capital, St John's, with its colourful, lively quayside, and the odd old-fashioned settlement like Parham or Old Road that progress seems to have bypassed. And if you're prepared to do a bit of walking, you'll find some superb hikes that will take you out to completely isolated parts of the island. As for nightlife, things are generally pretty quiet, though a good crop of restaurants – look out for those serving fresh West Indian cooking, especially seafood – do double duty as bars and dance clubs.

Meanwhile, Antigua's sister island **Barbuda** feels a world apart from its larger, more developed neighbour, even though it's less than 50km away and easily accessible by plane or ferry. With its spectacular, largely deserted beaches and pristine coral reefs, it may come as some surprise that tourism here is as low-key as it is – which is all the more reason to visit.

Antigua & Barbuda
AT A GLANCE

ST JOHN'S

Tucked into an inlet on the northwest coast, St John's most likely won't be why you come to Antigua, but to miss out on the city's great restaurants, entertaining commercial quays and vibrant daily life would be a shame. Be sure also to check out the cathedral, the national museum, the market and the waterfront.

▲ Entrance to St John's Cathedral

THE NORTHWEST COAST

Just north of St John's, this coast holds two well-manicured tourist areas; quiet Runaway Bay and more-developed Dickenson Bay. Both offer lovely beaches, shelving gently down into turquoise waters – visit Runaway for relaxed swimming and strolling, and Dickenson for watersports, eating and drinking.

▲ Runaway Bay

THE ATLANTIC COAST

The underdeveloped Atlantic coast is Antigua at its wildest and most natural state: deserted islands, abandoned sugar plantations and a lengthy stretch of rough, but incredibly scenic, coastline are all big draws for those willing to explore off the beaten track.

◄ Sugar mill

▲ Falmouth and English Harbour

FALMOUTH AND ENGLISH HARBOUR

Though not the best spot for good beaches, Falmouth and English Harbour contain most of the island's top sights. The nicely restored Nelson's Dockyard is a clear window to Antigua's colonial past, while several outstanding hikes, colonial forts, fine restaurants and lively bars will keep you plenty busy.

▲ West Coast palm trees

THE WEST COAST

Antigua's west coast features several major tourist developments along with some relatively deserted beaches. Highlights include Darkwood Beach, great for snorkelling and beachcombing; the massive Jolly Harbour resort and entertainment complex; and scenic Fig Tree Drive with its nearby hikes into hillside forests.

▲ White Bay in Barbuda

BARBUDA

Forty-eight kilometres north of Antigua, the island of Barbuda is perfect for those seeking unspoilt nature and laid-back West Indian culture. It's likely you won't see another soul lounging with you on the beaches, scuba diving the coral reefs or viewing the colony of frigate birds.

REDONDA

Near-impossible to reach, Redonda is a small chunk of volcanic rock populated only by goats and seabirds. Still, the story of how it came to be claimed as an independent kingdom is delightfully weird; see p.106 for more.

Ideas

The big six

There are a handful of places on Antigua that will give you a fully rounded picture of the country's rich **colonial history** – in essence the best of what's worth seeing beyond the countless beaches. A comprehensive tour takes you all around the island, from the capital city to the ruins around Falmouth and English Harbour to the rolling countryside along the island's Atlantic coast. To complete your impression, it's worth hanging around for either of the two main **festivals** that help define the nation in the eyes of the world.

▲ Sailing Week

One of the world's premier sailing events, attracting mariners from across the globe – but you don't have to be a yachtie to enjoy the parties.

P.77 ▶ FALMOUTH AND ENGLISH HARBOUR

▼ Betty's Hope

The island's most prominent sugar plantation for more than two hundred years and now the only working sugar mill in the Caribbean.

P.64 ▶ THE ATLANTIC COAST

▶ Nelson's Dockyard

Nelson called Antigua "this infernal hole", but his name has been borrowed for this beautifully restored Georgian dockyard.

P.75 ▶ FALMOUTH AND ENGLISH HARBOUR

◀ Shirley Heights

A visit to the Heights offers the chance not only to explore military history but also to enjoy wonderful views and, on Sunday, to party at *The Lookout*.

P.79 ▶ FALMOUTH AND ENGLISH HARBOUR

▶ Carnival

Beginning in late July, Antigua – St John's especially – is consumed by Carnival, which sees a week and a half of non-stop music and dance, culminating in a spectacular costume parade.

P.40 ▶ ST JOHN'S

▼ St John's

Don't miss this vibrant West Indian city with a lovely twin-towered cathedral, old wooden buildings, a lively market and shopping scene and a restored waterfront area.

P.35 ▶ ST JOHN'S

Beaches

Most visitors to Antigua head straight for the **beach** and, as a result, the most popular and developed ones can get especially crowded. While the west and northwest coasts see calmer seas, the winds and frequent swells on the Atlantic coast make for great bodysurfing, windsurfing and, for the really energetic, kiteboarding. Several strips also have great options for lunch on the beach, notably the superb west-coast stretch that takes in Darkwood Beach and Turner's Beach.

▼ Dickenson Bay

A beautiful half-mile stretch of white-powder sand and calm waters offering a fine choice of hotels, restaurants, bars and watersports.

P.52 ▶ THE NORTHWEST COAST

▼ Green Island

Take a boat trip to this peaceful and unin-habited island where you can stake out your very own strip of sand.

P.66 ▶ THE ATLANTIC COAST

▶ Rendezvous Bay

One of the most difficult beaches to reach on the island, but well worth the hike for the fine sand, the calm waters and the solitude.

P.72 ▶ FALMOUTH AND ENGLISH HARBOUR

◀ Pigeon Beach

The best beach around Falmouth and English Harbour, especially good for snorkelling and simply kicking back with a book.

P.78 ▶ FALMOUTH AND ENGLISH HARBOUR

▶ Darkwood Beach

This wonderfully quiet beach on the west coast features fine swimming and snorkelling, while nearby OJ's is probably Antigua's best beach bar.

P.93 ▶ THE WEST COAST

▼ Half Moon Bay

This beautiful crescent bay must be a contender for one of the loveliest beaches in the Caribbean, if not the world.

P.66 ▶ THE ATLANTIC COAST

Restaurants

Antigua features a growing selection of top-quality **restaurants**, showcasing great chefs and cuisine from around the world, as well as superb local **ingredients**, particularly those freshly pulled from the ocean. Most of the classy places are away from the big hotels and all-inclusives, but it's well worth getting out to them. You can also enjoy tasty fare at local spots like *George* and the *Roti King* in St John's, or *Caribbean Taste* and *Grace Before Meals* in English Harbour. For a true homegrown dining experience, sample the appetizing wares of street food vendors, found throughout St John's and at large construction sites around lunchtime.

▲ **Home**

Chef Carl Thomas' childhood home on the outskirts of St John's, where he and his German wife Rita now serve first-rate West Indian food.

P.47 ▶ ST JOHN'S

▲ **Coconut Grove**

Waterfront open-air thatched restaurant, known for its sensational seafood, at the *Siboney Beach Club.*

P.58 ▶ THE NORTHWEST COAST

▶ **Chez Pascal**

Outstanding traditional French cuisine served in a lovely Mediterranean setting in the hills of Five Islands Peninsula.

P.95 ▶ THE WEST COAST

▲ **Sheer**

With a magnificent cliff-top location and a menu of Asian/South American fusion, this *Cocobay Resort* restaurant compares with anything you'll find in New York or London.

P.100 ▶ THE WEST COAST

◀ **Harmony Hall**

The perfect spot for a long Italian lunch, perhaps taking a couple of hours' beach break on nearby Green Island before dessert and coffee.

P.69 ▶ THE ATLANTIC COAST

▶ **Papa Zouk**

Lively little spot on the outskirts of St John's offering generous bowls of delicious Creole seafood and a superb selection of rums.

P.47 ▶ ST JOHN'S

Colonial forts

The British, who ruled Antigua for over three centuries, left behind numerous **military fortifications**. Many were first built when the British and French navies were contesting the islands of the Caribbean in the 1660s and several were enlarged or strengthened during the Napoleonic wars. They must have been an effective deterrent since they never saw any further action, instead becoming signal stations, reporting on the movement of ships in the vicinity. The majority are now pretty dilapidated, though they all still command great views.

▲ Dow's Hill Fort

These rather limited ruins are in a superb location high above English Harbour, with a small multimedia museum nearby that summarizes the island's history.

P.81 ▸ FALMOUTH AND ENGLISH HARBOUR

▼ Fort James

Just north of St John's, Fort James is one of the island's best-preserved military installations. It's also right near the popular Fort Bay beach.

P.51 ▸ THE NORTHWEST COAST

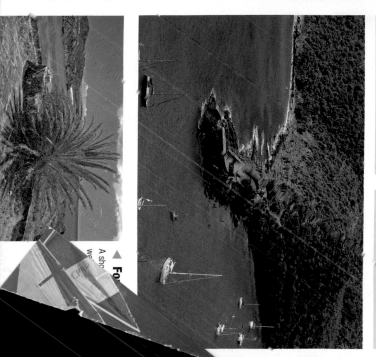

▲ Great Fort George

Extensive ruins high in the hills above Falmouth and English Harbour; you'll only make it up here on foot or by four-wheel drive.

P.72 ▸ FALMOUTH AND ENGLISH HARBOUR

▼ Fort Berkeley

These small but atmospheric ruins provide a great view of the entrance to English Harbour, and are just a short stroll from Nelson's Dockyard.

P.77 ▸ FALMOUTH AND ENGLISH HARBOUR

▲ Fo

A sho
we

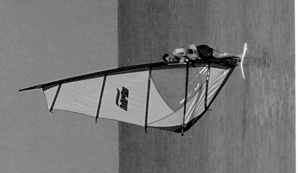

...y of **...rsports**. Just ...offshore, you can ...uise, sail, kayak, snorkel, bodysurf, windsurf, kiteboard, water ski, jet ski or swim with stingrays. Further out, you can try your hand at deep-sea sport fishing, going after wahoo, tuna, marlin and other sailfish. Underwater, you'll discover some spectacular dive sites, with coral canyons, caves and shipwrecks, home to all kinds of tropical fish and other marine creatures.

▲ Windsurfing on Dickenson Bay

One of the busiest strips of beach on the island, but the wind and waters are perfect for windsurfers, whether you're experienced or just starting out.

P.52 ▶ THE NORTHWEST COAST

◀ Kiteboarding at Jabberwock Beach

Try this exciting new sport if you dare: KiteAntigua has introduced it to a windswept beach on the island's Atlantic coast.

P.62 ▸ THE ATLANTIC COAST

◀ Kayaking eco-tours

Explore the island's hidden reefs, inlets and mangrove swamps by kayak with "Paddles" Kayak & Snorkel Club.

P.123 ▸ ESSENTIALS

▲ Sailing with Sunsail Club Colonna

Sunsail has the best equipment and a prime location for dinghy sailing – particularly good for getting kids out on the water.

P.68 ▸ THE ATLANTIC COAST

▶ Boating with Wadadli Cats

Catamaran cruises are a great way to explore the island's coast, snorkel the offshore reefs or simply relax with a rum punch.

P.123 ▸ ESSENTIALS

Antiguan specialities

You can find well-prepared versions of most of the big international cuisines on Antigua, but be sure to also try some of the **local specialities**. Fresh seafood and exotic fruit and vegetables are in abundance, and it's worth tasting them cooked in the traditional West Indian style. Look out, too, for the national fruit, the succulently sweet Antiguan black pineapple, as well as delicious regional dishes like ducana, fungi, souse and a variety of curries. Wash it all down with local beer and rum-based cocktails.

▲ **Wadadli beer**
The Carib Indians called the island Wadadli, now the name of the local brew.

P.119 ▸ ESSENTIALS

▼ Fresh fruit and vegetables

The public market in St John's is one of the best places for sampling the island's fresh fruit and vegetables.

P.44 ▶ ST JOHN'S

▲ Rum

Antiguan rums include the English Harbour and Cavalier brands, served in bars throughout the island.

P.119 ▶ ESSENTIALS

▼ Pepperpot stew

Made with salt beef, pumpkin and okra, this is a favourite dish in homes across the island.

P.47 ▶ FALMOUTH AND ENGLISH HARBOUR

▲ Market fish

Freshly caught fish is often the best menu option, with snapper and jack in particularly plentiful supply.

P.44 ▶ ST JOHN'S

Museums and galleries

A handful of small **museums** around the island neatly pull together Antigua's history. You'll find fascinating perspectives on the pre-Columbian period, the early European settlers and the boom years of British colonialism, dominated here by the sugar industry and the slave trade, and followed by emancipation and the road to national independence. There are also several excellent **galleries**, showcasing the work of artists and craftsmen from Antigua and elsewhere in the Caribbean.

▲ National Museum of Antigua and Barbuda

A lovingly assembled collection of exhibits on the island's past and present, from Arawak artefacts to a famous cricket bat.

P.41 ▶ ST JOHN'S

▼ Betty's Hope

The museum at this restored sugar mill recalls, through various tools and drawings, the time when sugar was King – and is a sobering reminder of the slave trade that made this possible.

P.64 ▶ THE ATLANTIC COAST

◀ **Harmony Hall**

The gallery at this restored plantation house (and outstanding Italian restaurant) shows art by top Caribbean artists and sculptors.

P.65 ▶ THE ATLANTIC COAST

▼ **Nelson's Dockyard Museum**

The world's only working Georgian dockyard includes a maritime museum that recounts the story of English Harbour.

P.75 ▶ FALMOUTH AND ENGLISH HARBOUR

▶ **Nick Maley's Island Arts Gallery**

Meet the creator of the *Star Wars* character Yoda at his downtown St John's gallery, close to where the cruise ships come in.

P.49 ▶ ST JOHN'S

Hikes

Dragging yourself away from the sand and sea may not be easy, but you'll find plenty of outdoor activities waiting if you do. **Hiking** is one of the most enjoyable of these: there are several interesting routes, with varying degrees of difficulty and the choice of going with a guide or solo. Many of the most frequented tracks and trails lead to various hilltops and fortifications, while others take you to beautiful beaches with few if any people around – the side of Antigua that most visitors don't see.

▼ Indian Creek

Look out over Eric Clapton's house and spectacular Willoughby Bay as you scramble steeply downhill to the creek.

P.82 ▶ FALMOUTH AND
ENGLISH HARBOUR

▼ Falmouth to Rendezvous Bay

It's about an hour's hike from Falmouth to the idyllic beach at Rendezvous Bay, or you can take the scenic route through the woodlands from Fig Tree Drive.

P.72 ▶ FALMOUTH AND
ENGLISH HARBOUR

▶ Wallings Woodlands

This forest reserve features some delightful nature trails – look out for mangoes, hog plums, passion fruit and lemongrass.

P.92 ▶ THE WEST COAST

▲ Middle Ground

West of Nelson's Dockyard, you can hike up onto this unusual peninsula for great views back across Falmouth and English Harbour.

P.78 ▶ FALMOUTH AND ENGLISH HARBOUR

◀ Boggy Peak

The communication station rather spoils the view of Boggy Peak, but the view back down certainly justifies hiking up to the highest point on the island.

P.92 ▶ THE WEST COAST

◀ Shirley Heights

Follow goat paths along cliffs and down to tide pools, and then clamber up a ridge with dramatic views of the rugged southern coast.

P.78 ▶ FALMOUTH AND ENGLISH HARBOUR

Entertainment and nightlife

You'll easily find ready-made evening **entertainment** at the big resort hotels. But if you're a little more adventurous, the non-packaged **fun** is usually better, especially around Falmouth and English Harbour. Shoot pool with sailors, get up and dance at various restaurants-cum-nightclubs or party with the locals to the latest Caribbean sounds. None of it may be particularly cutting-edge but, preceded by a few cocktails on the beach, this should be all the excitement you need.

▲ Liquid Nightclub and Grand Princess Casino

At the Jolly Harbour entertainment complex, this is the newest and largest nightspot on the island, with facilities for the casino enthusiast, too.

P.100 ▸ THE WEST COAST

◀ Abracadabra

Tuck into southern Italian food and once you've finished eating, hit the dance floor for the latest house music or live bands.

P.85 ▸ FALMOUTH AND ENGLISH HARBOUR

▶ The Rasta Shack

Relaxed, unassuming bar that livens up with the after-hours crowd who come for the cold Red Stripe and reggae music.

P.89 ▸ FALMOUTH AND ENGLISH HARBOUR

▼ The Lookout

Sunday is party time up on Shirley Heights when crowds of locals and visitors gather to enjoy reggae and steel bands.

P.82 ▸ FALMOUTH AND ENGLISH HARBOUR

◀ Life

Perched on a wooden pier right across the street from *Abracadabra*, this place has just as much action, but with a Sixties and Seventies musical bent.

P.87 ▸ FALMOUTH AND ENGLISH HARBOUR

Great views

Beyond the sunshine, the year-round warm temperatures and the fabulous beaches, Antigua is blessed with many other exquisite natural phenomena, including lush tropical vegetation, dramatic rock formations and some choice lookout points with panoramic **views** of the island. Make it a priority to explore some of these splendid sights, perhaps by renting a car for a day or two, asking a taxi driver to give you a full tour or taking an organized excursion.

▼ Fig Tree Drive

This drive through the most lushly forested part of the island offers some great views but no figs: it's the Antiguan word for bananas.

P.90 ▸ THE WEST COAST

▲ Hawksbill Rock

About half a mile offshore, this huge rock bears a striking resemblance to the head of a hawksbill turtle, the most endangered species of sea turtle.

P.97 ▸ THE WEST COAST

▶ Shirley Heights Lookout

The best place on the island to watch the sunset, whether or not you get to see the legendary "green flash".

P.79 ▸ FALMOUTH AND ENGLISH HARBOUR

◀ Devil's Bridge

Over the centuries, Atlantic breakers have carved a natural limestone arch and blowholes where surf crashes up and through.

P.65 ▸ THE ATLANTIC COAST

▶ Pillars of Hercules

Rarely seen by non-sailors, these spectacular natural columns of rock are so impressive that they serve as an aid to navigation for passing ships.

P.80 ▸ FALMOUTH AND ENGLISH HARBOUR

Barbuda

Just 48 kilometres north of Antigua lies **Barbuda**, the nation's other inhabited island. Chief among its attractions are the stunning and often deserted white-sand beaches, but it's also a great place for scuba diving and birdwatching, notably for a rare colony of frigate birds. The island has a colourful history, particularly during its two hundred years of ownership by the Codrington family. But you'll really want to come here to get away from it all: Barbuda is close to being the ultimate Caribbean escape.

▲ Palm Beach and Palmetto Point

Dreamy stretches of pink and white sand which, more often than not, you can have to yourself.

P.104 ▸ BARBUDA

▲ Spanish Point

There's little evidence of things Spanish on this southeastern tip of the island, but a spectacular marine reserve – Palaster Reef – lies just offshore.

P.106 ▸ BARBUDA

▶ Martello tower

Once the heart of the island's defences and still a great lookout spot to survey the island and surrounding ocean.

P.106 ▶ BARBUDA

◀ Codrington

The only settlement on Barbuda has a relaxed vibe – and is refreshingly uninflenced by tourism.

P.101 ▶ BARBUDA

▶ Caves

Take a break from the beach to explore the caves in Barbuda's Highlands, several of which are decorated with ancient carvings.

P.104 ▶ BARBUDA

▼ Frigate bird sanctuary

The Caribbean's largest nesting colony of these fabulous and unusual birds is a must for twitchers.

P.103 ▶ BARBUDA

Places

St John's

With a population of around 30,000 – nearly half the island's total – bustling St John's is Antigua's capital and only city. While not the prettiest town, it does have a certain immediate charm and offers a glimpse into everyday life in a typical West Indian community. The centre has plenty of attractive old wooden and stone buildings – some of them superbly renovated, others in a perilous state of near-collapse. An afternoon should be enough time for sightseeing, exploring back streets and shopping, but try to spend at least one evening in the city to sample some of its charming restaurants.

While in town, don't miss small but noteworthy National Museum, the city's twin-towered cathedral and Redcliffe Quay, where the waterfront and its colonial buildings have been attractively restored. Redcliffe Quay and nearby Heritage Quay are your best bets for souvenirs although you may want to avoid these areas if the cruise ships are in, when the steel drums come out to play Bob Marley standards for the throngs of shoppers.

Redcliffe Quay

By the waterside at the western end of Redcliffe Street. Redcliffe Quay is a good place to start your tour of the city. Named in honour of the church of St Mary Redcliffe in the English port city of Bristol, this is one of the oldest

Practicalities

As all of the main places of interest in St John's are close together, the easiest way to see the city is **on foot**. If you'd rather use your car, be advised that **driving** around town is straightforward if not particularly enjoyable; parking space is limited, the one-way traffic system a little tricky to deal with and potholes and roadside rain gullies threaten damage to your car at every turn. There are **taxi** stands just west of the market at the southern end of town, beside the East Bus Station and at Heritage Quay.

If you're arriving in or leaving the city by **bus**, keep in mind that the East Bus Station serves the north and the east of the island, while the West Bus Station, next to the market, serves the west (Dickenson Bay, Five Islands) and south (Jolly Harbour, Old Road, Falmouth and English Harbour).

For general **tourist information** visit the small booth at the centre of Heritage Quay or the Tourism Hospitality Unit on the second floor of the vendors' mall, #25 Heritage Quay (☎ 562 6944/5). They both have free road maps and a smattering of island brochures. To find out about any big **events** going on while you're in town, you'll need to rely on flyers, the newspaper, radio and word of mouth.

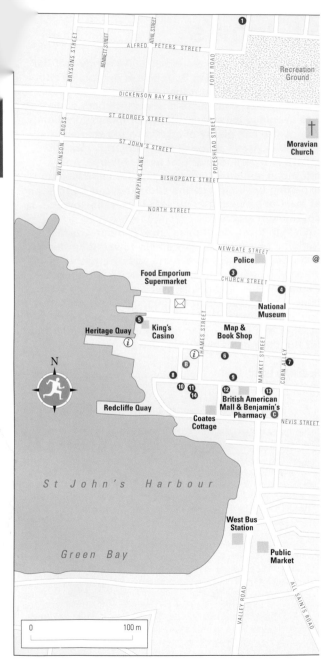

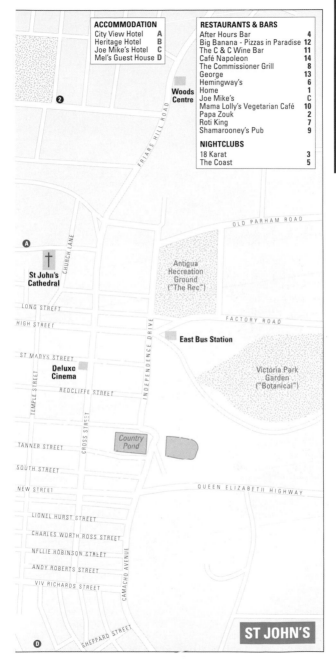

ACCOMMODATION	
City View Hotel	A
Heritage Hotel	B
Joe Mike's Hotel	C
Mel's Guest House	D

RESTAURANTS & BARS	
After Hours Bar	4
Big Banana - Pizzas in Paradise	12
The C & C Wine Bar	11
Café Napoleon	14
The Commissioner Grill	8
George	13
Hemingway's	6
Home	1
Joe Mike's	C
Mama Lolly's Vegetarian Café	10
Papa Zouk	2
Roti King	7
Shamarooney's Pub	9

NIGHTCLUBS	
18 Karat	3
The Coast	5

Woods Centre

❷

St John's Cathedral

CHURCH LANE

LONG STREET

HIGH STREET

FRIARS HILL ROAD

OLD PARHAM ROAD

Antigua Recreation Ground ("The Rec")

FACTORY ROAD

East Bus Station

ST MARYS STREET

Deluxe Cinema

REDCLIFFE STREET

TEMPLE STREET

INDEPENDENCE DRIVE

Victoria Park Garden ("Botanical")

CROSS STREET

Country Pond

TANNER STREET

SOUTH STREET

NEW STREET

QUEEN ELIZABETH II HIGHWAY

LIONEL HURST STREET

CHARLES WORTH ROSS STREET

NELLIE ROBINSON STREET

ANDY ROBERTS STREET

VIV RICHARDS STREET

CAMACHO AVENUE

SHEPPARD STREET

ST JOHN'S

▲ ST JOHN'S HARBOUR

parts of St John's, and incorporates many old warehouses – now attractively restored as small boutiques, nice restaurants and bars – and a wooden boardwalk that runs alongside the water. There's not a whole lot to see, but these several acres are a pleasant place to wander and soak up some of the city's history.

Many of the waterfront warehouses here once held supplies for the British navy and local merchant ships that traded between Antigua and the mother country during the eighteenth century – barrels of sugar and rum, lumber for ship repairs, cotton and sheepskins. The area behind the quay around the western end of Nevis Street held a number of barracoons, compounds where slaves were held after they arrived on the island and before they were sent off to the plantations or shipped on to other Caribbean islands.

Built on the side of one such barracoon is the recently restored Coates Cottage, a tiny white wooden structure with black trim and a few small rooms with high pointed ceilings. It serves as an art gallery, and if they're open they'll let you into the small brick walled courtyard out back where the slaves were once held before they were sold. It's overgrown with creeper vines and bougainvillea and adorned with rusted tools and birdcages, beautiful but eerie, especially considering its history. The adjacent wooden building used to be a bargaining house, where auctions were held and slaves sold off to loca estate-owners.

Heritage Quay

By the waterside at the western end of St Mary's Street. This modern concrete quay is given over to cruise-ship arrivals and dozens of duty-free shops designed to catch the tourist dollars, along with local vendors selling T-shirts and toy steel drums. Unless you're shopping there's little reason to stop by except for a quick look at the Westerby

Memorial Fountain, which commemorates a Moravian missionary dedicated to helping Antiguans in the decades after emancipation from slavery in 1834.

King's Casino

Heritage Quay ☎ 462 1727, ⓦ www .kingscasino.com, Mon–Sat 10am– 4am, Sun 6pm–4am. Mostly electronic gambling machines with a few blackjack, roulette and Caribbean stud poker tables. Live bands and karaoke on weekends give this otherwise worn-down and dim place a bit of atmosphere. The casino offers one-way shuttle services for those coming for the night. It'll pick you up anywhere, but you'll be stuck with the taxi fare home – so make sure you don't lose it all.

The Rec

Eastern end of Long Street. Modest and unassuming as it looks, the Rec is one of the finest cricket pitches in the Caribbean. With its outfield and wicket lovingly tended by trusted inmates from the nearby prison, it looks at quiet times like any cricket pitch in England or Australia. Don't believe it for a moment. On match days, while the rest of the island comes to a standstill, the Rec is transformed into a cacophonous whirligig, with music belting from the stands, men on stilts and women in wigs, and hordes of vendors flogging jerk chicken and cold beer.

If you've got any sense of adventure, head for Chickie's Double Decker stand at the north end of the ground. With his banks of huge speakers tied to the railings, the eponymous DJ blasts everyone within earshot with the songs of local Calypsonians, and they all sing along to the chorus of "Rally Round the West Indies". Bumping and grinding away, more intent on the beer and the chat-up lines than the cricket, the happy spectators will be there long after stumps have been drawn and the players have retired to the pavilion. Cricket season runs from January to July, when the Rec shifts gears to become the main stage for summer Carnival festivities.

Victoria Park Botanical Garden

Behind the East Bus Station. Sunrise to sunset. Free. This formerly neglected park is undergoing a

▲ HERITAGE QUAY

Carnival

The highlight of Antigua's entertainment calendar is **Carnival**, an action-packed ten-day party held from late July until the first Tuesday in August. Warm-ups start in early July, with steel bands, Calypsonians and DJs in action across the island, while Carnival proper gets cracking with the opening of Carnival City at the Rec (see p.39). This is where all the scheduled events take place, though you'll often find spontaneous outbreaks of partying across the city. A festival village is set up nearby to provide space for the masses of food and drink vendors who emerge out of nowhere.

The major Carnival events take place over the last weekend, when you'll feel compelled to forgo sleep for a few days of frantic action. The Panorama steel band contest (Friday night) and the Calypso Monarch competition (Sunday night) are both packed and definitely worth catching, while on Monday morning – the day on which the islands celebrate slave emancipation in 1834 – Jouvert (pronounced "jouvay", and meaning daybreak) is a huge jump-up party starting at 4am. The Judging of the Troupes and Groups competition in the afternoon sees ranks of brightly costumed marching bands and floats parading through the city streets, being marked for colour, sound and general party attitude.

On Tuesday there's a final costumed parade through the streets, finishing with the announcement of all of the winners and a roughly 6pm–midnight last lap from Carnival City – "the bacchanal" – as the exhausted partygoers stream through St John's, led by the steel bands. All in all, it's an excellent event: certainly one of the best of the Caribbean's summer carnivals, and a great chance to catch Antiguans in a non-stop party mood.

Visit Antigua Carnival's website (ⓦwww.antiguacarnival.com) for a "scrapbook" of last year's Carnival and a complete program of the upcoming summer's festivities with details of this year's bands.

major revitalization and offers a pleasant escape from the hustle and bustle of downtown. It sits on the highest hill around – a perfect spot to enjoy cool breezes on a hot day. You'll find picnic tables under a giant ficus tree,

where you can tuck into some of the local foods for sale around the East Bus Station. Many of the trees are labelled but botanical enthusiasts may want to first visit the "Natural" section of ⓦwww.antiguamuseums.org for

▼ CLAPBOARD HOUSE

a map of the park and descriptions of the trees, which include mahogany, lignum vitae (whose wood is so dense it does not float on water), strangler fig and the curious sausage tree.

The National Museum

Corner of Long and Market streets ☎ 462 1469, ⊛ www .antiguamuseums.org. Mon–Fri 8.30am–4pm, Sat 10am–2pm. EC$8 donation.

▲ RURAL ANTIGUAN COTTAGE, THE NATIONAL MUSEUM

Housed in a 1750 Neoclassical courthouse, the National Museum of Antigua and Barbuda is indisputably worth visiting while you're exploring the capital – you can almost feel the enthusiasm with which the collection has been assembled and displayed. The exhibits start by showing off the islands' early geological history, backed up by fossils and rock samples, and move on to more extensive coverage of their first, Amerindian inhabitants. Jewellery, primitive tools, pottery shards and religious figures used by these early settlers have been found at sites across Antigua and Barbuda and are well exhibited here.

The museum has small displays on Columbus, the European invasion and sugar production. An interesting 1750 map of Antigua shows the plantations, as well as all the reefs that threatened shipping around the island. There is also an unusual exhibit on the emancipation of the slaves and the resulting patterns of settlement. Upon emancipation in 1834 there were only four towns on Antigua, with almost all the ex-slaves living on the sugar estates; the planters usually refused to sell them land, since they wanted to keep them tied to the plantations. The exhibit shows how – either with the assistance of missionaries or by sheer determination – the former slaves were able to set themselves up in "free villages" across the island.

Elsewhere, there are displays on the island of Barbuda, which might whet your appetite for a visit (see p.101), and the tiny uninhabited rock of Redonda (see p.106). You'll also find an example of the ancient game of *warri* or *mancala*, brought by slaves from Africa's Gold Coast, and a touch and feel section with stone and shell tools. Last but certainly not least, one of the museum's most prized exhibits is the cricket bat with which, in 1986, Antiguan Vivian Richards (now Sir Vivian) scored the fastest-ever test-match century, taking just 56 balls to score 100 runs against England on his home turf (see box, p.42). The museum offers a guide to St John's historical buildings and architectural styles, well worth picking up for your strolls about town. For those wanting to dig deeper into the island's history, there's also a research library. The small gift shop has locally made paintings, crafts and hot sauces, as well as reproduction maps of the islands, postcards and books.

St John's Cathedral

Newgate Street, west of Church Lane. Daily 9am–5pm. Donations appreciated. The imposing twin towers of the Cathedral Church of St John the Divine are the capital's dominant landmark. A simple wooden church was first built on this hilltop site in 1681 and, after heavy destruction was wrought by a number of earthquakes and hurricanes, the present cathedral was put up in 1847.

From the outside, the grey-stone Baroque building is not particularly prepossessing – it's squat and bulky, and the two towers are capped by slightly awkward cupolas. More attractively, the airy interior of

Cricketing heroes

The first Antiguan to play for the West Indies team was fast bowler **Andy Roberts**, who made his debut against England in 1974; he was shortly followed by **Vivian Richards**, who first played against India in the same year. Within a couple of years both players had made a dramatic impact – and were heavily involved in the slaughter of English cricket in 1976. In 1981 the island was awarded the right to stage its first test match, where Richards made the superb century discussed in the National Museum account (see p.41).

It's hard to overestimate the importance of Vivi (as he's known locally) to the development of the country's self-confidence in the years immediately before and after independence in 1981. For this tiny island to have produced a man rated by many as the finest batsman of his generation was an enormous boost to its self-esteem. Throughout his career, Richards' spectacular hitting and imperious manner endeared him to a generation of cricket-watchers worldwide. Now retired, Richards has eschewed the political career many expected, but the street where he was born in St John's now bears his name (it runs east–west just south of the public market), and a new large cricket stadium is being built in his name in the centre of the island (curiously by Chinese workers on a grant from China). As a "goodwill ambassador" he remains one of Antigua's most precious living assets.

Though unthinkable just two decades ago, today tiny Antigua is one of the leading cricketing venues in the Caribbean, with test matches, Busta Cup and Red Stripe Cup games played there annually. Between 1985 and 1995 the West Indies team was captained by Antiguans – Richards and, later, his protégé Richie Richardson – and Antiguan players like fast bowler Curtly Ambrose and wicketkeeper Ridley Jacobs have continued to feature prominently. Small wonder, perhaps, that at times people appear to talk of little else.

▲ VIVI RICHARDS' BAT

▲ ST JOHN'S CATHEDRAL

the cathedral is almost entirely encased in dark pine, designed to hold the building together in the event of earthquake or hurricane. The walls are dotted with marble tablets commemorating distinguished figures from the island's history, some of them rescued from the wreck of earlier churches on this site and incorporated into the new cathedral. In the grounds of the cathedral, the whitewashed and equally Baroque lead figures on the south gate – taken from a French ship near Martinique in the 1750s during the Seven Years' War between France and Britain – represent St John the Baptist and St John the Divine, draped in flowing robes.

Independence Avenue

Independence Avenue commemorates, at least in name, the long struggle for Antiguan nationhood. There are not necessarily any reminders of this past – just a collection of drab office buildings and residences and a constant flow of traffic – but you'll almost certainly find

yourself on this road at some point, en route to somewhere more interesting. Still, the story itself is compelling.

By the time of World War II, life for the vast majority of Antiguans was very tough. There was widespread poverty and unemployment across the island, while for those who did work on the plantations, hours were long and conditions onerous. In 1938, the Moyne Commission was sent from London to report on social conditions in the West Indies, and recorded that Antigua was among the most impoverished and neglected islands in the region. The commission recommended reform to the island's stringent laws banning trade unions, and in the following year the Antigua Trades and Labour Union (ATLU) was formed.

Within a few years the Union had helped to improve conditions for plantation workers. Its major success came in 1951 when, under the leadership of former Salvation Army officer Vere (V.C.) Bird,

▲ FRESH FRUIT

workers refused to handle the sugar crop until their rates of pay were improved. For a year, the employers tried to starve the workers into submission, but they were eventually forced to concede a substantial pay rise. Subsequently, national confidence began to improve.

After the war, Antigua continued to be administered from afar by Britain's colonial office, but gradually the island's fledgling politicians were given authority for the day-to-day running of their country. The Antigua Labour Party, an offshoot of the ATLU, won the first local elections in 1946, and a decade later the island was given responsible ministerial government (meaning that the local people formed the government, though ultimate authority still lay with Britain). Ideological differences between the political parties – there were a variety of small parties, in addition to the larger ALP – were minimal, and all parties quickly came to support some form of independence from Britain. A constitutional conference was held in 1966,

leading the following year to autonomy for the country in its internal and foreign affairs, although defence remained a matter for Britain.

Slowly, the national economy began to take strides forward, assisted (despite the closure of the last sugar plantations in 1971) by the development of tourism. By the elections of 1980 all parties considered that, politically and economically, the country was sufficiently mature for full independence and, following a further conference in Britain, the flag of an independent Antigua and Barbuda was finally raised on November 1, 1981. Since then, each year on this day an Independence Day Parade takes place at the Rec (see p.39).

The public market

At the south end of Market Street. Mon–Sat from around 6am until sunset. Home to the colourful public market, Market Street was once known as Scotch Row, in honour of the traders – many of them early Scottish immigrants – who once lined it with shops selling sugar, indigo, coffee, tobacco and rum.

Today it remains an important shopping thoroughfare, and is particularly lively on Friday and Saturday. It's housed in a new brightly painted building, the envy of other West Indian cities. In addition to local fruits, flowers and vegetables, you'll find locally made woven and knit crafts. The bustling fish market is just across the street, in front of the buses. If you're hungry, pick up some delicious soursop, pineapples or mangoes when they're in season or check out the cheap local eateries behind the market.

The V.C. Bird statue

Right outside the public market is a large statue of V.C. Bird, who dominated Antiguan politics for half a century after taking over the leadership of the ATLU in 1943. Known as Papa Bird, he became the colony's first chief minister in 1956, its first premier in 1967, when internal self-government was granted by Britain, and the first prime minister of an independent Antigua and Barbuda in 1981.

Though Bird has long been hugely popular with Antiguans, he and his entourage have also been consistently controversial. During his time in power, his government developed a reputation for doing business with all kinds of dodgy characters. There were allegations that ministers had brokered arms deals between Israel and the apartheid regime in South Africa, and even with the Medellin drug cartel in Colombia. A British commission accused the government of "unbridled corruption", and the US – who kept a military base on the island and poured in over US$200 million in aid – of turning a blind eye, in an era when fear of radical governments (such as those of Cuba and Grenada) was the United States' leading concern.

Whatever the truth of the allegations, Vere Bird retained power until 1994 when, at the age of 84, he handed leadership of his party and the country to his giant son Lester, once Antigua's leading fast bowler and now probably its wealthiest man.

Accommodation

City View Hotel

Newgate Street ☏ 562 0256, ⨍ 562 0242, ⓦ www.cityviewhotelantigua.com. City centre hotel aimed at the business traveller, with 39 spacious, air-conditioned rooms, with cable TV, kitchen and balcony for US$129 single and US$164 double (price includes tax and breakfast). Ask for a view room for vistas of the town and harbour.

Heritage Hotel

Heritage Quay ☏ 462 1247, ⨍ 462 1179, ⓦ www.heritagedowntown.com. Right by the cruise-ship pier, this hotel is a decent option if you're in town on business; otherwise, it's completely missable. Spacious uninspired rooms, each with their own well equipped kitchens and priced from $154 (including tax and breakfast).

Joe Mike's Hotel

Corner of Nevis Street and Corn Alley ☏ 462 1142, ⨍ 462 6056, ⓔ joemikes@candw.ag. The dozen

▼ V.C.BIRD STATUE

rooms in this friendly, central spot are small but decent with TV and a/c. There's a lounge area, a small casino and a popular restaurant in the building (See opposite for a review of *Joe Mike's* eatery). Rooms cost US$71 single or double.

Mel's Guest House

Corner of All Saints and Sheppard streets ☎764 1250. A short walk south from the downtown market and bus station, this small, easy-going (though uninspiring) guesthouse has clean rooms with private baths and fans. One of the cheapest options on the island, charging US$46 per night. Ask for a room away from the busy street.

Restaurants and bars

After Hours Bar

Corner of Corn Alley and Church Street ☎562 4740. Mon–Fri 4.30–12pm, Sat 7pm–late. No cover. This upstairs, laid-back lounge is colourfully lit and features a pool table, some outdoor seating, and good pumping reggae and house music.

Big Banana – Pizzas in Paradise

Redcliffe Street ☎480 6985 or 480 6986, ☎480 6989, ⊛www.bigbanana-antigua. com/pizzas.html. Mon–Sat 8.30am–midnight. Popular with tourists for lunch and dinner, this pub-like spot serves food of reasonable quality – pizzas, pastas and salads,

as well as more traditional Antiguan fish and chicken meals. Prices are decent, from EC$15 to EC$60.

Café Napoleon

Redcliffe Quay ☎562 1820. Mon–Sat 8.30am–3.30pm. At this French-owned and -styled café/patisserie, enjoy good breakfasts – freshly baked baguettes and croissants with butter, jam, pineapple juice and coffee for EC$17 – and, at lunchtime, excellent sandwiches (EC$24 – 45) on a shaded patio.

The C&C Wine Bar

Redcliffe Quay ☎460 7025. Daily 10am–late. This lovely grotto with outdoor tables specializes in South African wines at US$3–10 per glass. They also serve cheese or paté platters for EC$20 and olives (EC$5). Their Friday night BBQ consists of Indonesian-style chicken and shrimp skewers for EC$30.

▼ HEMINGWAY'S

The Commissioner Grill

Between Redcliffe and Heritage quays ☎ 462 1883. Daily 10am–11pm. Excellent West Indian food is served all day in this popular and easy-going saloon, from tasty breakfasts of saltfish, eggs or fruit to hearty suppers of fish, chicken and lobster (EC$40–85).

George

Corner of Market and Redcliffe streets ☎ 562 4866, ✉ george@actol.net. Daily 8.30am–11pm. In the heart of the city, this lively restaurant serves top-notch West Indian food on a large, airy upstairs gallery decked with sea-blues and -greens. The regular menu includes fire-roasted jerk shrimp and "chicken on a wire" (EC$35), while on Saturdays they offer a number of Antiguan specialities including goat water, conch water, souse, rice pudding and pepperpot stew (EC$15–25).

Hemingway's

St Mary's Street ☎ 462 2763, ⊛ www .hemingwaysantigua.com. Mon–Sat 8.30am–11pm. Housed in an early nineteenth-century green-and-white wooden building, with a balcony overlooking the street and Heritage Quay. It can get very crowded when the cruise ships are in, but at other times, it's a relaxing place to be, with a range of excellent food, from sandwiches and burgers to fish and steak dinners (EC$20–68).

Home

Gambles Terrace, Lower Gambles ☎ 461 7651, ⊛ www .thehomerestaurant.com, ✉ ritagohome@hotmail.com. Mon–Sat dinner only. Closed June & July. Attractive restaurant in a converted home, a little ways from the centre of town, serving

▲ CREOLE BOUILLABAISSE AT PAPA ZOUK

"Caribbean haute cuisine". Look for tasty starters of crab cakes (EC$26–34), elaborate main courses of fillet of snapper stuffed with shrimps in lobster sauce (EC$65), blackened jackfish in chilli garlic sauce (EC$55) or chicken breast with fresh mango and pineapple in a coconut curry sauce.

Joe Mike's

Corner of Nevis Street and Corn Alley ☎ 462 1142. Daily 7.30am–11pm. Unpretentious local eatery and small hotel (see p.45) that's a popular lunchtime haunt for government officials and other prominent Antiguans. Servings include large portions of ducana and saltfish, stewed pork, fungi and lingfish, all for around EC$15–25.

Mama Lolly's Vegetarian Café

Redcliffe Quay ☎ 562 1552. Daily 9am–9pm. Small, friendly café serving fresh-pressed juices and smoothies for EC$10–15, and also veggie burgers, tofu stir-fry and their popular veggie wraps for EC$10 to EC$23 including salad.

Papa Zouk

Hilda Davis Drive, Gambles ☎ 464 6044. Mon–Sat 7–11pm. This

eclectic Creole seafood restaurant pleases the ears with festive French Caribbean Zouk music, the eyes with its colourful patio, festooned with hanging plants and bright tablecloths, and the palate with large portions of delicious seafood dishes like Creole bouillabaisse or a whole pan-fried snapper (EC$25–50). The bar features over 180 different rums and the sociable owner is happy to discuss them with you. Try their Ti Punch, a wonderful homemade rum punch that is also available to go in bottles. No credit cards. Reservations suggested.

Roti King

St Mary's Street ☎ 462 2328. Daily 8.30am–1am. Housed in a cute traditional home with just five plastic tables, this local eatery

serves tasty Trinidadian fare (starting at EC$12), including daily curries and roti (a soft flaky thin bread wrapped around curried potatoes and vegetables or meat). Try it with the tart tamarind sauce. Wash it all down with homemade drinks of fresh-squeezed lime, tamarind, guava, ginger and sorrel (when in season) for EC$3. At lunchtime you'll see rastas, policemen and schoolgirls all munching on their yummy rotis.

Shamarooney's Pub

Redcliffe Street ☎ 775 5199. 10am–11pm. Popular Irish pub with a European crowd, football on the telly and karaoke on Wednesday nights.

Street vendors

Usually only around lunchtime, vendors set up throughout town, at bus stations and at construction sites. This can be an inexpensive way to sample tasty, home-cooked Antiguan fare. Look for the silver catering trailers in town, or women on the side of the road, selling pepperpot stew, goat water and saltfish with fungi, ducana or rice and peas for EC$10 to EC$15 (for descriptions of these, see p.119). Fruit vendors sell bananas, freshly cut sugarcane, sugared tamarind balls, fresh mangos and pineapples when in season.

▼ CRAFT MARKET

Shops

British-American Mall

Redcliffe Street. Mon–Sat 8.30am–6pm. A mini-mall above Benjamin's pharmacy with an herbal health vendor, a shop called Made in Antigua that sells local handicrafts, jams and paintings and an excellent bookstore, Best of Books, with a large selection of novels, international newspapers and magazines.

Food Emporium Supermarket

At the bottom of Long Street by the water. Mon–Thurs 8am–7pm, Fri & Sat 8am–10pm, Sun 8am–4pm. This large supermarket is a good spot to pick up inexpensive eats to go.

Island Arts Gallery

Heritage Quay ☎462 2787, ⓦwww .yodaguy.com. Mon–Fri 9am–5pm, Sat 9am–4pm. One of the more noteworthy stores at Heritage Quay. The owner, British painter Nick Maley, was originally a film make-up artist who worked on movies such as *Star Wars* (for which he created the Yoda character). He has now lived on Antigua for over twenty years, and this small gallery is crammed with his paintings and prints, as well as those of Antiguan, Haitian and other West Indian artists.

The Map & Book Shop

St Mary's Street. ☎462 3993. Mon–Fri 9am–5pm, Sat 9am–2pm. Great little bookstore carrying most books published in Antigua, including some unique children's books, historical perspectives and poetry. They also carry a comprehensive selection of natural history field guides, Caribbean travel books, sailing guides, maps of the island and reproductions of antique maps.

National Museum Gift Shop

Corner of Long and Market streets ☎462 1469. Mon–Fri 8.30am–4pm, Sat 10am–2pm. Small, interesting shop with locally made pottery, cards, artwork, hot sauces, books and even a few antiques.

Woods Centre

Friar's Hill Road, 750m north from the junction of Cross and Newgate streets. At this American-style shopping centre, you'll find The Epicurean, the island's best-stocked supermarket (daily 8am–10pm), as well as banks, a pharmacy, a Radio Shack, a post office, a travel agent, an office supply store, a FedEx, a Western Union and a local artists' cooperative gallery (see below).

Woods Gallery

Woods Centre ☎462 2332, ⓦwww .antigua-artist-gallery.originalcarib-beanart.com. Mon–Sat 10am–5.30pm. Featuring the artwork and crafts of over 40 Antiguan artists, a new exhibit opens on the first Thursday evening of each month with wine, cheese and the local art crowd. Check their website for a listing of artists, an online store and a schedule of exhibitions.

Entertainment and nightlife

18 Karat

Church Street ☎562 1858. Thurs–Sun 10pm–late. Cover EC$20. Popular with young Antiguans, this clubbing hotspot plays mostly Hip Hop and R&B. Thursdays and Sundays ladies get in free and gents pay EC$10.

The Coast

Heritage Quay, next to King's Casino. New nightclub with a deck on the water and current Hip Hop and R&B hits. Sundays and Wednesdays are the big nights.

Deluxe Cinema

High Street ☎ 462 2188. Ticket prices EC$15–20, kids EC$8. The island's only cinema, showing the latest American films to an interactive audience.

The northwest coast

Most of Antigua's visitor development has happened along this coast, which boasts long stretches of calm, sunwashed beaches. Just north of St John's, Fort Bay has a good public swath of sand with parking, and at its southern end, the notable historical site of Fort James, one of the best-preserved colonial forts on the island. A little further north, Runaway Bay is being developed on its northern and southern ends but is otherwise a mostly deserted beach with great swimming. Above this lies Dickenson Bay, one of the island's main tourist strips, with an excellent beach backed by a host of good hotels, restaurants and bars. Behind Runaway and Dickenson bays is McKinnon's Salt Pond, fringed by mangroves and busy with birdlife.

Fort Bay

Fort Bay is home to a long, wide strand of grainy white sand that's packed with city-dwellers at weekends and holidays. At its northern end, you can hire beach chairs from *Millers*, which is also a good place to pick up a drink (see review, p.58).

At the southern end of the strip, a host of food and drink stalls open up at busy times, transforming the place into a lively outdoor venue, with music blaring, fish frying and plenty of frolicking on the beach. If you want to swim, there's a protected, marked area at the top of the beach; elsewhere, though the water is normally fine, you'll need to watch out for occasional undercurrents.

▼ CANNON AT FORT JAMES

Fort James

Together with Fort Barrington (see p.94) and St John's Fort on Rat Island, the eighteenth-century Fort James was designed to deter any ships from attacking the capital, which had been sacked by French raiders in 1666. Though earthworks were first raised here in the 1680s, the bulk of the fort wasn't

▲ RUNAWAY BAY

put up until 1739, when the long enclosing wall was added. The place never actually fired a shot in anger, although its guns undoubtedly intimidated visiting vessels into paying the eighteen shillings levied to the fort's captain.

Today, though the fort is pretty dilapidated, it still offers plenty of interesting structures for poking around and great views across the channel and back down to St John's harbour. Rusting British cannons from the early 1800s point out to sea and down the channel, their threat long gone but still a dramatic symbol of their era. Elsewhere, the old powder magazine is still intact, though leaning precariously, and the stone buildings on the fort's upper level – the oldest part of the structure, dating from 1705 – include the master gunner's house, the canteen and the

barracks. Today, part of the fort houses the atmospheric *Russell's* restaurant (see p.58).

Runaway Bay

Quiet Runaway Bay features gleaming white-sand beaches that slope gently down into the turquoise sea. Great for calm swimming, Runaway Bay has fewer hotels to tidy up their "patch" of sand than the built-up Dickenson bay, and so is strewn with more seaweed and rocks. Still, it's a great place to wander in the gentle surf, though at the northern end much of the beach has been eroded by heavy swells.

Corbison Point

Just in front of the *Marina Bay Hotel*, grassy Corbison Point pokes out into the sea, dividing Runaway Bay from Dickenson Bay. A stone powder store is the sole remnant of an eighteenth-century British fort that once stood here. The cliff has also yielded Amerindian potsherds and evidence that ancient island-dwellers exploited flint in the area for their tools. You may see holes in the ground, dug by artefact poachers.

Dickenson Bay

Trapped between two imposing rocky bluffs, Dickenson Bay is fringed by a wide white-sand beach, which stretches for over a

▼ CORBISON POINT

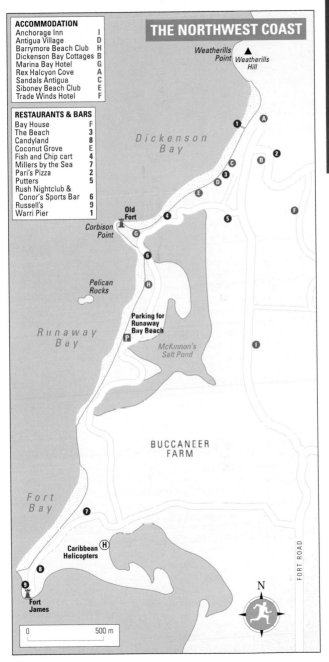

THE NORTHWEST COAST

ACCOMMODATION
Anchorage Inn	I
Antigua Village	D
Barrymore Beach Club	H
Dickenson Bay Cottages	B
Marina Bay Hotel	G
Rex Halcyon Cove	A
Sandals Antigua	C
Siboney Beach Club	E
Trade Winds Hotel	F

RESTAURANTS & BARS
Bay House	F
The Beach	3
Candyland	8
Coconut Grove	E
Fish and Chip cart	4
Millers by the Sea	7
Pari's Pizza	2
Putters	5
Rush Nightclub & Conor's Sports Bar	6
Russell's	9
Warri Pier	1

Weatherills Point
Weatherills Hill

Dickenson Bay

Old Fort
Corbison Point

Pelican Rocks

Parking for Runaway Bay Beach

Runaway Bay

McKinnon's Salt Pond

BUCCANEER FARM

Fort Bay

Caribbean Helicopters

Fort James

FORT ROAD

N

0   500 m

kilometre between Corbison Point and the more thickly vegetated woodland of Weatherills Hill at its northern end. It's a lovely bay, shelving gently into the sea and with protected zones dividing swimmers from the jet-skiers, windsurfers and waterskiers who frolic further offshore.

▲ DICKENSON BAY

The northern half of the beach fronts some of the largest of Antigua's hotels, including the *Rex Halcyon Cove*, whose pier juts out into the sea and offers dining above the ocean, and *Sandals*, with its striking yellow pavilions (see p.56 for reviews of these hotels). The area can get pretty busy, particularly in high season, with bars, hair-braiders and T-shirt sellers doing a brisk trade. Still, it remains an easy-going place, with minimal hassle.

McKinnon's Salt Pond

McKinnon's Salt Pond encompasses over 200 acres of brackish water edged by mangroves. More than 25 species of water birds have been recorded here, in particular sandpipers, snowy egrets, terns and plovers that nest on the sand (much of which is sadly being converted into a jogging path) and redfooted herons that breed in the mangroves. There are no nature trails, and since many birds are quite close to shore the best way to view them is to stroll the pond's perimeter. Encroaching developments and the stench of raw sewage give one the impression that this ecosystem is not particularly valued by the government – and there is talk that this wetland will be converted into a marina for powerboats.

Birdwatching

With an estimated 120 species of birds, up from 87 in the 1930s, Antigua is a great place to rise with the sun, strap on the binoculars and go **birdwatching**. You can spy plenty of seabirds at **McKinnon's Salt Pond** (see above) and at most beaches around the island. Watch out in particular for pelicans, showing off their clumsy but spectacular technique of divebombing for fish. Other good birdwatching spots include **Wallings Woodlands** (p.92), with red-necked pigeons, broadwinged hawks and Antillean bullfinches; the **Potswork Reservoir**, in the centre of the island, with pied-billed grebes, West Indian whistling ducks and grey kingbirds; **Fitches Creek Bay** (p.63); and **Barbuda** (p.101). For more information on birdlife in Antigua, visit the National Museum's website ⊛ www.antiguamuseums.org. You can also arrange to go birdwatching with museum-recommended guides, Junior Prosper (☎ 773 1159) or Victor Joseph (☎ 775 1495, ✉ vjosephlib@yahoo.com), who charge from US$30 to US$50 per person depending on the destination. The Environmental Awareness Group (☎ 462 6236) occasionally leads birdwatching hikes on the third weekend of the month.

Accommodation

Anchorage Inn

Anchorage Road ☏ 462 4065, ⓕ 462 4066, ⓦ www.antiguaanchorageinn .com. Just north of St John's, this cosy, brightly painted hotel with a small pool lies about a kilometre from the beach and caters to business travellers and visiting medical students. US$95 for a double room.

Antigua Village

Dickenson Bay ☏ 462 2930, ⓕ 462 0375, ⓦ www.antiguavillage.net. Unremarkable resort with dozens of self-catering apartments – from studios to two-bedroom flats, starting at around US$290/175 in winter/ summer – strewn about attractively landscaped gardens. The beach has been replaced by a stone seawall to slow erosion, but there are very nice beaches to either side of it. You'll also find a small swimming pool and a grocery store (8am–6pm) with fresh produce. It's close to several good restaurants.

Barrymore Beach Club

Runaway Bay ☏ 724 7618. This quiet spot sits on a small piece of land with its own tiny, secluded beach. The studios and apartments are comfortable if unspectacular – ask for one close to the sea. The well-kept gardens bloom with hibiscus and feature all types of palm. One- and two-bedroom apartments range from US$355/205 to US$240/135 per night.

Dickenson Bay Cottages

Dickenson Bay ☏ 462 4940, ⓕ 462 4941, ⓦ www.dickensonbaycottages .com. Thirteen spacious, airy and attractively furnished cottages are set around a well-landscaped garden and medium-sized pool, up on a hillside overlooking Dickenson Bay. It's a quiet place but just a short walk from all the action on the beach. One-bedroom cottages cost US$160/140 for two people in winter/summer (US$46 per additional person, kids under 12 stay free). Two-bedroom cottages cost US$305/250 for up to four.

Marina Bay Hotel

Dickenson Bay ☏ 462 3254/8, ⓦ www .marinabayantigua .com. On the southern end of

▲ MCKINNON'S SALT POND

▲ SIBONEY BEACH CLUB

Dickenson Bay, just behind Corbison Point, lies this complex of apartments on a small marina. The units range from spacious and bright studios to large rooms with four beds. All have a kitchen, TV, a/c, private balcony and bathtubs. The mediocre landscaping and lack of pool may disappoint some, but the rooms are well-maintained, there is a quiet beach, and the prices are low at US$115/95 for a studio and US$225/185 for a two-bedroom unit.

Rex Halcyon Cove

Dickenson Bay ☎ 462 0256, ⓕ 462 0271, ⓦ www.rexcaribbean.com. Large, sprawling low-rise resort with vintage late-sixties architecture featuring good-sized rooms, a great beach, friendly staff, decent pool, tennis courts and a restaurant on Warri Pier (see review p.59). Rooms start at US$280/230.

Sandals Antigua

Dickenson Bay, ☎ 462 0267, ⓕ 462 4135, ⓦ www.sandals.com. Part of the popular, all-inclusive chain found throughout the Caribbean, this resort has 193 luxury rooms with another 180 suites on the way. The original rooms are cleverly spread throughout the resort, reducing the sense of being part of a large crowd of guests. The new rooms, however, are in a large, hotel-style concrete building. Five restaurants offer excellent Italian, Japanese, southern US, bistro grill and international food, and all watersports (no jet skis), including diving (certification costs extra), are included. Priced from around US$365 per person per day.

Siboney Beach Club

Dickenson Bay ☎ 462 0806, ⓕ 462 3356, ⓦ www.siboneybeachclub.com. Small, intimate and friendly place, fabulously landscaped in a micro-jungle with its own white-sand beach and a garden pool. Rooms are spacious and comfortable, and one of the island's best restaurants (*Coconut Grove*; see p.58) is on site. The friendly owner Tony Johnson has been living in Antigua since the 1950s and has a wealth of information about the island. A suite – which includes bedroom, lounge with TV, kitchenette and patio or balcony – costs from US$190/130 in winter/summer. The choicest ones are right up in the jungle "canopy" with ocean views.

Trade Winds Hotel

Dickenson Bay ☎ 462 1223, ℱ 462 5007, ⊕ www.antiguatradewindshotel .com. Lovely place in the hills above the bay, with big, comfortable air-conditioned rooms. Guests can chill out by the lagoon pool on a wide veranda overlooking the ocean or take the regular shuttle down to the beach, a kilometre away, where sun loungers are freely available. The hotel's *Bay House* restaurant (see review, below) has fine food and great views. Double rooms start at US$225/195 in winter/summer.

Restaurants and bars

Bay House

At the *Trade Winds Hotel*, Dickenson Bay ☎ 462 1223. Daily 7am–11pm. This smart restaurant, on an airy terrace high on the hill overlooking Dickenson Bay, is a romantic spot for a sunset drink followed by top-flight food. Creative,

tasty starters set the tone – tuna nicoise (EC$30) or scallops wrapped in prosciutto (EC$32), for example – while main courses include coconut and pineapple lobster (EC$75), quail with plum sauce (EC$68) or rack of lamb with a rosemary port sauce (EC$85). Lunch is also a good option with fine sandwiches, salads, pastas, seafood and steaks (EC$20–70).

The Beach

Dickenson Bay ☎ 480 6940, ℱ 480 6943, ⊕ thebeach@candw.ag, ⊕ www .bigbanana-antigua.com/beach.html. Daily 8.30am–midnight. Brightly painted restaurant on the beach right by the *Antigua Village* (see review, p.55), serving good food all day. Lunches include sushi, pizzas, burgers and salads served for EC$20–50, while dinner specials could include sesame-crusted tuna, meat-topped pasta or seafood stew for EC$45–85. Often has entertainment on the

▼ THE BEACH

weekends (see "Nightlife", opposite).

Candyland

Fort James ☎ 460 5304. Daily 9.30am–8pm. Friendly little beach bar under the Casuarina trees just before you reach Fort James, serving good, simple food and cold drinks all day long. Regular specials include various curries, steamed fish and conch chowder, all for around EC$25–35.

Coconut Grove

At the *Siboney Beach Club*, Dickenson Bay ☎ 462 1538, ℻ 462 2162, ℮ coconut@candw.ag, ⊛ www .coconutgroveantigua.com. Daily 7.30am–11pm. Great cooking and friendly service combine at this delightful open-air beachside location. Mouthwatering starters include coconut shrimp in a coconut dip (EC$34), followed by main dishes of *mahi mahi* in a mango sauce (EC$70) and rock lobster drizzled in Creole sauce (EC$85). For dessert, try the magnificent coconut cream pie (EC$25). Worth a visit for the social beach bar.

Fish and chip cart

Dickenson Bay ☎ 724 1166. Wed & Fri 4–9pm. If you're craving a round of fish (or sausage) and chips, look out for the catering trailer parked on the main road between the *Marina Bay Hotel* and *Siboney Beach Club* most Wednesday and Friday evenings. A basket of fried fish, shrimp or lobster and chips will run you EC$25–40, sausage and chips EC$15, Indian curry with rice and naan bread and meat pies EC$25.

Millers by the Sea

Fort Bay ☎ 462 9414. Daily 8am–11pm. Large, but often empty, beachside restaurant with an extensive menu. Typical dishes include curried conch or pan-fried snapper for EC$45, and there's normally a beach barbecue for lunch and dinner on Monday. Occasionally they'll have evening entertainment such as karaoke or a DJ. Happy hour Mon–Fri 5–7pm.

Pari's Pizza

Dickenson Bay ☎ 462 1501. Tues–Sun 5.30–11.30pm. This spot is all about pizzas, ribs and steaks – slightly overpriced at EC$65 for a small rack of ribs, EC$28 for the smallest of the pizzas, and EC$80 for the surf and turf. Reasonable enough if you're staying nearby, though.

Putters

Dickenson Bay ☎ 463 4653. Food daily 11am–midnight, bar open till 2 or 3am. Fun place with lively music on a large outdoor covered deck. Mostly British comfort food like steak & kidney pie, curries and burgers (including veggie) for EC$22 – 35. Appetizers and small pizzas start at EC$12. There is a small playground for kids, a few pool tables and a fully lit mini-golf course costing EC$10 to play.

Russell's

Fort James ☎ 462 5479. Daily 11am–10pm. This airy, classy restaurant is in a colonial-era fort and features spectacular views. The small menu focuses on seafood, and includes appetizers of whelks in garlic sauce and conch fritters for EC$30 and main dishes of the catch of the day and grilled lobster for EC$45–75. They host live jazz on Sundays from 2–9pm.

Warri Pier

At the *Rex Halcyon Cove*, Dickenson Bay ☎ 462 0256. Daily 11am–11pm. Open-air dining on a colourfully painted pier jutting out into the bay. American staples dominate the lunch menu, with reasonably priced burgers and BLTs, while the evening menu is more creative, with fresh fish and steaks for US$20–35.

Nightlife

The Beach

Dickenson Bay ☎ 480 6940, ℉ 480 6943, © thebeach@candw.ag, Ⓦ www .bigbanana-antigua.com/beach.html. On Tuesday nights a live music duo engages the crowd, leading crab races and giving away prizes. Friday is the big night with a DJ (10.30pm–2am; EC$10 cover) and on Saturdays there is a live band from 4pm to 9pm (no cover charge) on a stage set up just outside the restaurant on the edge of the beach.

Conor's Sports Bar

Runaway Bay ☎ 562 7874. No cover charge. Sharing a large building with *Rush Nightclub*, this bar has pool tables, dartboards and a nice balcony overlooking the water. Simple pub food includes burgers, salads and pizzas (EC$10–30) and there's a two-for-one happy hour daily from 5pm to 7pm. Open 5pm until late.

Rush Nightclub

North end of Runaway Bay, in the same building as *Conor's* ☎ 562 7874. One of the latest island hotspots. Thursdays and Sundays are retro- and salsa-themed respectively (EC$10 cover), and more casual than Friday and Saturday nights, which require smart elegant attire when the R&B, Hip Hop and international music gets cranked up (EC$30 cover). Friday is the big night with a mixed crowd of locals and tourists. Open from 11pm to 5am but doesn't get going till late.

The Atlantic coast

Continuing east around the island from the top of Dickenson Bay brings you to Antigua's Atlantic coast. Here, the long jagged coastline, from Boons Bay to Half Moon Bay, offers plenty of inlets, bays and swamps – but, with a couple of noteworthy exceptions, rather less impressive beaches.

Though tourist facilities on this side of the island are much less developed, there are still several places of interest. Betty's Hope is a partially restored sugar plantation; Parham, the island's first port, has a lovely old church; Devil's Bridge offers one of the most dramatic landscapes on the island; at the delightful Harmony Hall, you can relax over an excellent lunch; and at picturesque Half Moon Bay, scramble along a vertiginous clifftop path above the pounding Atlantic.

Hodges Bay

For the most part, Hodges Bay is a high-end residential area, though it does have a few good restaurants including *Le Bistro* and *The Cove* (see p.69) and an excellent family-oriented hotel in *Sunsail Club Colonna* (see p.68). If you want to make use of the latter's enormous swimming pool or top-quality sailing equipment – Hodges Bay is great for sailing, as strong winds typically blow across this north coast spot – day passes are generally available, at US$50 for a full day or US$25 for a half. There's also a good dive shop

▲ SAILING AT HODGES BAY

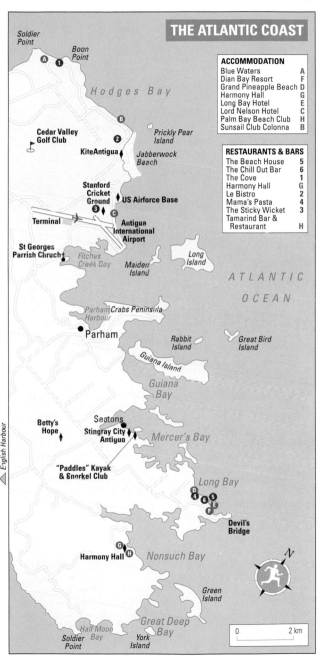

THE ATLANTIC COAST

ACCOMMODATION
Blue Waters	A
Dian Bay Resort	F
Grand Pineapple Beach	D
Harmony Hall	G
Long Bay Hotel	E
Lord Nelson Hotel	C
Palm Bay Beach Club	H
Sunsail Club Colonna	B

RESTAURANTS & BARS
The Beach House	5
The Chill Out Bar	6
The Cove	1
Harmony Hall	G
Le Bistro	2
Mama's Pasta	4
The Sticky Wicket	3
Tamarind Bar & Restaurant	H

▲ STANFORD CRICKET GROUND

here called Ultramarine, offering the usual packages for certified or non-certified divers as well as "surface scuba" for children between 5 and 12 years old; see p.122 for contact info. As for the beach itself, it's decent, but not particularly good for hanging out – rather, this part of the island is best for watersports fanatics (see also Jabberwock Beach, below).

Prickly Pear Island
Five minutes' boat ride from the beach at Hodges Bay. Prickly Pear Island is a small, uninhabited place with a nice beach and good snorkelling. On Tuesdays, Thursdays and Saturdays, a friendly character named Miguel runs day trips out here from the beach at Hodges Bay for US$65 or US$35 for kids (☎460 9978 or 772 3213, ⓦwww.pricklypearisland.com). The price includes sunbeds, snorkelling gear and all-you-can-eat and -drink from a big buffet-style lunch of seafood and West Indian specialities.

Jabberwock Beach
This decent little public strip of sand doesn't match up to the highly manicured beaches in front of the island's resorts, but it is totally undeveloped, free of crowds, and has plenty of parking. Because of its strong winds and relative seclusion it has become the home to the island's first kiteboarding operation, KiteAntigua (☎460 3414 or 727 3983, ⓦwww.kiteantigua.com). This new sport combines some of the principles of windsurfing, wakeboarding and just plain flying: a rider on a board controls a huge, partly inflated kite so that it pulls him along the water and often several feet into the air. Even if it sounds too extreme a sport (or indeed, too expensive – a 4hr beginner's course will set you back a whopping US$200), it's well worth stopping to watch for a while. Call ahead to arrange for lessons or equipment.

Stanford Cricket Ground
Right by the airport, amid some major new developments including banks, restaurants and a health club, you'll find the Stanford Cricket Ground, a spectacular new floodlit stadium with a pavilion, stand and

cricket-themed restaurant, *The Sticky Wicket* (see review, p.70). The stadium doesn't host test matches (these will still be played at the Rec in St John's; see p.39) though it does serve as a practice pitch for international touring teams, as well as the venue for local day or night matches. Call *The Sticky Wicket* (☎481 7000) to find out if anyone is playing.

Fitches Creek Bay

Fitches Creek Bay is a desolate inlet with no beaches of note, dotted with brackish mangrove swamps. It's a great birdwatching spot: look out for herons, egrets and whistling ducks among the multitude of local species. For other birdwatching sites, see the box on p.54.

St George's Parish Church

Overlooking Fitches Creek Bay, St George's Parish Church was first constructed in 1687 – though hurricane and earthquake damage have each long since taken their toll. Recent reconstruction of the place is largely complete, the church having been gutted and a new roof raised, but the ancient, weathered brick walls and crumbling tombs facing out to sea still lend it a strong sense of history.

St Peter's Anglican Church

First settled in the seventeenth century, Parham, one of the oldest inhabited towns on the island, boasts the impressive, octagonal St Peter's Anglican Church, considered unique in the Caribbean. A wooden church was first erected here in 1711, although the present structure mostly dates from 1840. The inside is spacious, with stained glass and an unusual wooden ribbed ceiling designed like an upturned ship's hull. The church is usually eerily quiet and isolated, except for the bats, birds and termites that now call it home. If the gates are closed, but not locked, you can let yourself in – though it might be nice to first ask permission of nearby residents who can usually fill you in on the church's history and local events.

Parham Harbour

Outside St Peter's Anglican Church, the cemetery tumbles down the hill towards Parham Harbour, Antigua's first port. Protected from the Atlantic waves by offshore islands, this fine natural anchorage was busy with ocean-going ships for more than two centuries until sugar exports slumped in the 1920s. Now it shelters a few yachts and small fishing vessels

▲ ST PETER'S ANGLICAN CHURCH

▲ BETTY'S HOPE

and there's a small jetty at the eastern end of town. If you're in the area, it's worth taking an hour or two to wander around this quiet waterfront that feels untouched by time.

Betty's Hope

Tues–Sat 10am–4pm or by appointment ☎462 4930.
Founded in the 1650s, the first and largest sugar plantation in Antigua was granted to the Codrington family of Barbados in 1674 and named after the daughter of Christopher Codrington, Governor General of the Leeward Islands. By the end of World War II, lack of profitability forced the closure of the historic plantation. Today, although most of Betty's Hope still lies in ruins, one of the windmills has been restored to working condition, and a small, interesting museum at the visitor centre tells the history of sugar on Antigua and explains the development and restoration of the estate.

St Stephen's Anglican Church

East along Collins Road, about 1.5km from Betty's Hope. The otherwise unremarkable St Stephen's Anglican Church has been rebuilt to a curious design, with the pulpit in the centre and the pews on each side. Meanwhile, outside the church, the crumbling tombs in the flower-strewn cemetery are testament to the fact that – in spite of the recent rebuild – the place has been a religious site for several centuries.

Seatons

The village of Seatons is the starting point for two very enjoyable, informative and well-organized ecotour attractions. The first, offered by Stingray City Antigua, allows you to swim with stingrays in their "natural" environment, a large penned area of ocean not far offshore (US$50 per person; T562 7297, ⓦwww .stingraycityantigua.com). The second, offered by "Paddles" Kayak & Snorkel Eco-Adventure, is a half-day kayak tour of the nearby islands, inlets and mangroves, with an option to hike to sunken caves and snorkel in the North Sound Marine Park (US$50 per person, US$35 for children aged 7-12; ☎463 1944, ⓦwww .antiguapaddles.com).

Devil's Bridge

1km east along track signposted off Collins Road. On a large barren limestone outcrop edged by patches of grass and tall century plants, Devil's Bridge takes its name from a narrow piece of rock whose underside has been washed away by thousands of years of relentless surf. The hot, windswept spot offers some great views, both over a quiet cove and across the surging ocean and dark reefs to a series of small islands just offshore.

En route back to the main road, a dirt track on your right after 400m leads down to a tiny but gorgeous bay – the perfect venue for a picnic. The place plays occasional host to some local parties, and can get rather litter-strewn, but the turquoise sea is exceptionally inviting and the usually empty strip of white beach a great place to chill out.

Long Bay

Though Long Bay is home to a couple of rather exclusive all-inclusives, the *Long Bay Hotel* and *Pineapple Beach* (see pp.67 & 68), this doesn't stop you from gaining access to a great, wide beach, enormously popular with local schoolkids, who can often be found splashing around or playing cricket at one end. The lengthy spread of white sand is protected by an extensive reef a few hundred metres offshore, so be sure to bring your snorkelling gear or rent some from Island Water Sports (☎774 6511), who also rent jet skis and will take you waterskiing. You'll also find a couple of beach bars and restaurants, good for shelter and refreshment when you've had enough sun.

Harmony Hall

The restored plantation house at is now home to a tiny, chic hotel (see p.67), one of the island's best restaurants (see p.67) and a great gift shop and art gallery that showcases exhibitions of local and Caribbean art from November through April. Though it's a ways away from the main tourist hangouts and a little awkward to reach (down some poor quality roads), it's a relaxed, friendly and delightful place, well worth the detour.

▲ DEVIL'S BRIDGE

Green Island

Five minutes' boat ride from the jetty at Harmony Hall. On deserted Green Island, the beaches are powdery and the snorkelling excellent. The island is privately owned, yet the beaches are free to use. There is no regular transport offered to Green Island, unless you are part of an island boat tour, or a guest at *Harmony Hall* (see opposite).

Half Moon Bay

One of the prettiest spots on Antigua, Half Moon Bay boasts a kilometre-long semicircle of white-sand beach partially enclosing a deep-blue bay, where the Atlantic surf usually offers top-class bodysurfing opportunities. The isolation of this side of the island means that the beach is often pretty empty, especially since the 1995 closure, after Hurricane Luis, of the expensive hotel at its southern end. Note that these remote roads are probably the best in the island, owing no doubt to the presence of the nearby private *Mill Reef Club*, so exclusive that you can't even visit their website without a password.

Soldier Point

At the southern end of Half Moon Bay, the headland of Soldier Point marks the beginning of an excellent 45min circular hike. Where the beach ends you can clamber up onto the rocks and a trail – marked by splashes of blue paint along its entire length – that cuts left along the edge of the cliff. It's a moderately tough climb, with a bit of a scramble required in places, but worth the effort for some fine views out to sea and over the bay and – apart from butterflies and seabirds – a sense of splendid isolation. Don't go barefoot, though: the rocks are sharp in places and there are plenty of thorns around.

Accommodation

Blue Waters

Blue Waters Bay ☎ 462 0290, ⓕ 462 0293, ⓦ www.bluewaters.net. Perched on its own picture-perfect bay with a lovely white-sand beach, this fine resort offers everything from suites to villas, all with rattan furniture, subdued colour schemes, individual bathrobes

▼ SAILING TO GREEN ISLAND

▲ HARMONY HALL

and water vistas. The crowd is rather upscale, but the resort still has all the fun stuff, like sailboats, several pools, and so on. Double rooms start at US$435/316 in winter/summer. Rates include breakfast and another US$225 per couple will get you lunch, dinner and drinks too.

Dian Bay Resort and Spa

Just past Long Bay Hotel ☎460 6646, ℱ460 8400, ⓦwww.dianbayantigua .com. This pastel, all-inclusive resort sports 50 identical rooms (only the view differs) from $400/250 winter/summer. It features all sorts of spa treatments, a three-tiered pool and a decent mini beach – and they also offer a free shuttle to an even better one nearby. Nice large bar and restaurant on the water, although reviews are mixed about the service and food quality. No children under 16.

Harmony Hall

Brown's Bay Mill ☎460 4120, ℱ460 4406, ⓔharmony@candw.ag, ⓦwww .harmonyhallantigua.com. A small, delightful Italian-run place in

the middle of nowhere, open from November to mid-May only. There are six simple but stylish rooms, which start at US$195, with tiled floors, large bathrooms, comfortable beds and small patios. The beach isn't up to much, but there's a nice small pool and a free shuttle boat regularly ferries guests out to the clean white sand at Green Island, five minutes away (see opposite). The restaurant (see p.69) is classy and normally busy; when it's closed (as it is at dinnertime during the week), the hotel can provide room service for guests. Don't come here for anything other than total peace and quiet.

Long Bay Hotel

Long Bay ☎463 2005, ℱ463 2439, ⓦwww.longbayhotel.com. Closed Sept & Oct. A small all-inclusive in a fabulous setting by a tiny turquoise bay, with twenty cosy rooms, five cottages and a real feeling of isolation. Although it can feel a bit outdated, the owner and his friendly staff pride themselves on keeping everything very low-key and relaxed. That said, there are a few sailboats and windsurfers, a good tennis court and a library and games room with table tennis. This may not be the place for young honeymooners, as an older crowd tends to stay here. Rooms start at US$355/267 in high/low season for two, including breakfast, dinner, taxes and gratuities.

Lord Nelson Beach Hotel

Dutchman Bay ☎462 3094 ⓦwww .lordnelsonantigua.com. The large, concrete bunker-style rooms are sparsely furnished and only have floor fans. However, the hotel does sit right on a decent little beach with palm trees and each room has a small private balcony overlooking the sand. There's usually a great breeze and this is probably the least expensive waterfront option on the island at US$100/85 winter/summer including breakfast. They share the beach with H2O Antigua, which offers windsurfing and sailing lessons and rentals (see p.124). The small restaurant serves three meals a day.

Occidental Grand Pineapple Beach

Long Bay ☎463 2006, ☎463 2452, ⓦwww.allegroantigua.com. Sprawling but attractively landscaped all-inclusive, with 180 rooms (US$500/460 in winter/summer) scattered alongside a lovely stretch of beach. The place can feel crowded, but the facilities – including four tennis courts, a fitness centre and free non-motorized watersports – are good and there are plenty of activities to distract you. Three restaurants mean you get a bit of variation for your meals, and in the evening you can choose between four bars including a piano bar.

Palm Bay Beach Club

Browns Bay ☎460 4174 ⓦwww .palmbayantigua.com. Closed Sept and Oct. A handful of small villas (sleeping 4-6) sit on a small peninsula with lots of grassy open spaces, some well-placed palm trees and a calm beach that's better for sunbathing than for swimming because of the seagrass beds just a few feet from the shore. They do, however, have a pool, tennis court and nice small restaurant (*Tamarind Bar & Restaurant*, see

▲ LE BISTRO

p.70) on the premises. The villas are decent with fans and mosquito netting over the beds and a small fridge and toaster oven. Rates start at US$240/180 per villa, or US$120/100 for a couple, including breakfast. This can be a good spot to stay with small children because of the calm water and large grassy lawn, but it's quite far from most of the island's attractions, and a 4WD vehicle is recommended for the bad roads.

Sunsail Club Colonna

Hodges Bay ☎462 6263, ☎462 6430, ⓦwww.sunsail.com. This attractive, watersports-themed resort is Mediterranean in design, with red-tiled roofs and pastel shades, plus the largest pool on the island. The hotel itself can get quite crowded, but their fleet of nearly a hundred sailboats and windsurfers, all with free lessons, make it easy to get away. Most guests take part in the windsurfing and sailing schools and many are with young ones – this is one of the most child-friendly hotels on the island, with kids' clubs for all ages. They also have adult-only weeks; check their website. You'll find a good dive shop, a new gym and a "body zone" for manicures, massages and so on. Room rates start at US$330/190 in winter/summer and all meals may be included if they're running a special, although their one restaurant feels like nothing more than a cafeteria with a view.

Restaurants and bars

The Beach House

At the *Long Bay Hotel*, Long Bay ☎ 463 2005. Daily for lunch only. Good selection of salads, sandwiches and fish (EC$25–40) at this casual terrace restaurant next to a beautiful stretch of beach. When cruise ships are in at St John's, it can get crowded for a couple of hours in the middle of the day, as many passengers are told that Long Bay has the best beach on the island, and that they should take a taxi ride over for a brief visit. BBQ every Thursday night.

The Chill Out Bar

Long Bay. Daily for lunch only. Often lively local spot right on the beach that makes for a great place to take a break from the sun and surf. Chicken and rice, burgers or fish and chips for EC$15–25.

The Cove

Blue Waters Bay ☎ 562 2683. Daily for dinner only; reservations recommended. This new upscale restaurant owned by the nearby *Blue Waters Resort* has proper linens, comfortable chairs and excellent service. It's

spectacularly lit at night with tiki torches on the outdoor veranda and floodlights on the sea, which you can catch glimpses of down a cliff. The food is equally stylish and includes starters (from EC$30) of goat cheese and red pepper tart and seared sea scallops with pancetta, and popular mains of rack of lamb with dijon crust (EC$95) and filet of sea bass with olive tapenade (EC$70).

Harmony Hall

Brown's Bay Mill ☎ 460 4120, ⓕ 460 4406, ⓔ harmony@candw.ag, ⓦ www .harmonyhallantigua.com. Daily 10am–6pm, Fri & Sat dinner also, closed May–Nov. Run by a charming Italian couple, this is one of the island's finer restaurants, even if it is in a remote spot. Built around an old sugar mill, the elegant but simple food is served on a terrace overlooking the bay. The menu includes starters of pumpkin soup (EC$20), homemade mozzarella with beetroots (EC$26) and an extraordinary *antipasto misto* (EC$35); mains of lobster tortellini (EC$38) or red snapper in a light cherry tomato and white wine sauce (EC$65); and delicious desserts of crème brulée (EC$18) or deep-fried bananas in cinnamon (EC$20). Despite the long drive along a road that's seen better days, the place is always busy and well worth the trip.

Le Bistro

Hodges Bay ☎ 462 3881, ⓕ 461 2996, ⓔ pgbistro@candw.ag. Tues–Sun dinner only. Long-established and well-reputed restaurant with a calm vibe and good, unobtrusive service. They serve excellent French cuisine, including starters of chilled apple curry soup for EC$24 and snails in garlic butter for EC$30, and mains of lobster medallions (EC$85), snapper in ginger white wine sauce (EC$70) and duck in orange sauce (EC$75).

Mama's Pasta

Long Bay ☎ 773 0527. Lunch and dinner; closed Tuesdays. This brightly painted beach shack is just atop the little hill at Long Bay beach. They serve great sandwiches and burgers for EC$10–18 and pastas and pizzas for EC$17–57.

The Sticky Wicket

Pavillion Drive (next to the airport), Coolidge ☎ 481 7000, ⓦ www .thestickywicket.com. Lunch and dinner daily. New cricket-themed diner and sports bar right next to the Stanford Cricket Ground (see p.62). Even outside the cricket season, there's a good buzz here, with regular live music, TVs showing top sporting events, unusual cocktails and excellent food. Bar snacks like West Indian pork ribs and spicy jerk buffalo wings go for around

EC$25, meat and fish mains cost EC$40–90 and there's a nice kids' menu for EC$15. Not worth the trip unless you're a cricket fanatic, but it can be a good place to wait for your flight, as it's right beside the airport terminal.

Tamarind Bar and Restaurant

Browns Bay ☎ 460 4174, ⓦ www .tamarindbarandrestaurant.com. Breakfast and lunch daily, dinner most nights. Call ahead. Closed Sept–Oct. Casual little spot just past *Harmony Hall* with an appetizing menu of fish soup Provençale EC$35, mussels with ginger and coriander EC$30 and catch of the day for EC$52. Having a meal here entitles you to use the waterfront facilities of the *Palm Bay Beach Club*: a tennis court, pool, kayak and trampoline. There is lots of open grass around here making it a good place to bring little kids for the afternoon. It is, however, rather far out, and the road is pretty bad.

Falmouth and English Harbour

An essential stop on any visit to Antigua, the picturesque area around Falmouth and English Harbour on the island's south coast holds some of the most important and interesting historical remains in the Caribbean; it's now also the region's leading yachting centre and a hotbed for nightlife. The chief attraction is the eighteenth-century Nelson's Dockyard, which was the key facility for the British navy that once ruled the waves in the area. Today it's a living museum where visiting yachts are still cleaned, supplied and chartered, with several ruined forts nearby, as well as an abundance of attractive colonial buildings now converted into shops, hotels and restaurants.

In the hills across the harbour from the dockyard, there is further evidence of Antigua's colonial past at Shirley Heights, where more ruined forts, gun batteries and an old cemetery hold a commanding position over the water. It's a dramatic place whose rather forlorn air is shattered on Sunday evenings when steel and reggae bands lend sound to a lively (if somewhat over-touristed) barbecue party.

The area also has a handful of far less visited spots that repay a trip, including Great Fort George, high in the hills above Falmouth; the seldom visited Pillars of Hercules; and Rendezvous Bay – outstanding in an area with a paucity of good beaches.

Getting to Rendezvous Bay

Heading out from Falmouth, turn left on Farrell Avenue and follow the road past the colourful Rainbow School onto a dirt track edged with banana groves. Take a right at the first intersection, past the Spring Hill Riding Club, then, at the fork, go left up a hill that soon becomes paved. There's a big, white house at the top of the hill; park near it and follow the track that veers off to the left. Driving a car, it should take around 5min to reach this point from the top of Farrell Avenue; on foot, it'll take about 25min.

The track climbs briefly between Cherry Hill and Sugar Loaf Hill, offering great views back over Falmouth Harbour, then drops down through the scrubby bush, with sea grape and acacia trees on either side. After 25 to 40 minutes you'll reach a rocky bay strewn with conch shells; a further 10- to 15-minute wander along the beach brings you to Rendezvous Bay.

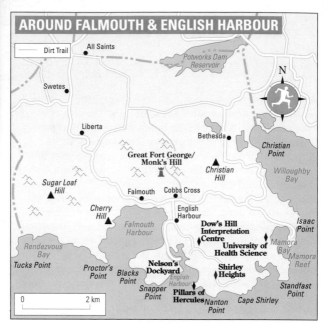

AROUND FALMOUTH & ENGLISH HARBOUR

Dirt Trail

All Saints

Potworks Dam Reservoir

N

Swetes

Liberta

Bethesda

Christian Point

Great Fort George/ Monk's Hill

Christian Hill

Willoughby Bay

Sugar Loaf Hill

Falmouth

Cobbs Cross

English Harbour

Cherry Hill

Falmouth Harbour

Dow's Hill Interpretation Centre

University of Health Science

Isaac Point

Mamora Bay

Mamora Reef

Rendezvous Bay

Tucks Point

Proctor's Point

Blacks Point

Nelson's Dockyard

English Harbour

Shirley Heights

Snapper Point

Pillars of Hercules

Nanton Point

Cape Shirley

Standfast Point

0   2 km

Falmouth Harbour

This large, beautiful natural harbour has been used as a safe anchorage since the days of Antigua's earliest colonists, and the town that sprang up beside it was the first major settlement on the island. Today, though the harbour is still busy with yachts, Falmouth itself is a quiet place, most of the activity in the area having moved east to the village of English Harbour.

Rendezvous Bay

Although there is no beach of particular note in Falmouth, you can make a great hike from just west of town to Rendezvous Bay, the most idyllic and one of the quietest beaches on Antigua (see the box on p.71 for directions). Caressed by an aquamarine sea, and backed by coconut palms and dotted with driftwood, this curve of fine

white sand is a gorgeous place to swim. The comparatively remote location means that there is rarely anyone else here, although the occasional boat trip makes its way across from Falmouth to use a thatched barbecue hut on the beach, which offers welcome shade. Bring some water, a picnic, a book and some snorkelling gear, and you could easily spend a day here.

Great Fort George

High above Falmouth, are the ruins of one of Antigua's oldest defences, Great Fort George (also known as Monk's Hill). The remains of the fort aren't much, but the spectacular panoramic views over the harbour and most of the rest of the island make this trip worth the effort. There's rarely anyone here – giving the visitor a quiet

▲ FALMOUTH HARBOUR

but evocative sense of the island's past.

The fort was constructed during the late seventeenth century, when England was at war with France. After the French navy captured the nearby island of St Kitts in 1686, the English decided to build Great Fort George on the hills behind the island's main town, together with housing and water cisterns to provide a secure retreat for Antigua's tiny population. Though the French never in fact invaded, the fort was eventually completed in 1705, with dozens of cannons pointing in all directions; barracks and gunpowder stores were added during the following century. By the mid-1800s, when any threat of invasion had receded, the fort was employed as a signal station, using flags to report on the movement of ships in and around Falmouth Harbour.

Upon arrival, you'll notice that much of the enormous stone perimeter wall remains intact. Meanwhile, inside the main gate and to the right, the west gunpowder magazine (built in 1731) has been well restored. It's fun to wander around the rest of the extensive overgrown and dilapidated ruins and see if you can identify which part was living quarters and which part military establishment. Wear long pants if you intend to bushwhack your way around.

To reach the fort, take the turnoff at Cobbs Cross toward Mamora Bay and make an immediate left on the small road beside the school. Bear left at the fork and continue up until your car can go no further, then continue by foot the additional twenty minutes to the fort. You might make it all the way in a 4WD vehicle. Alternatively, from Liberta (north of Falmouth; see p.83), take the inland road to Table Hill Gordon, from where

Practicalities

A **car** is invaluable for touring around this area of the south coast. There are frequent buses between St John's and English Harbour, handy if you just want to explore Nelson's Dockyard, but to get up to Shirley Heights you'll certainly need your own transport or a taxi. See the listings on p.114 in Essentials for car rental, tours and taxi information.

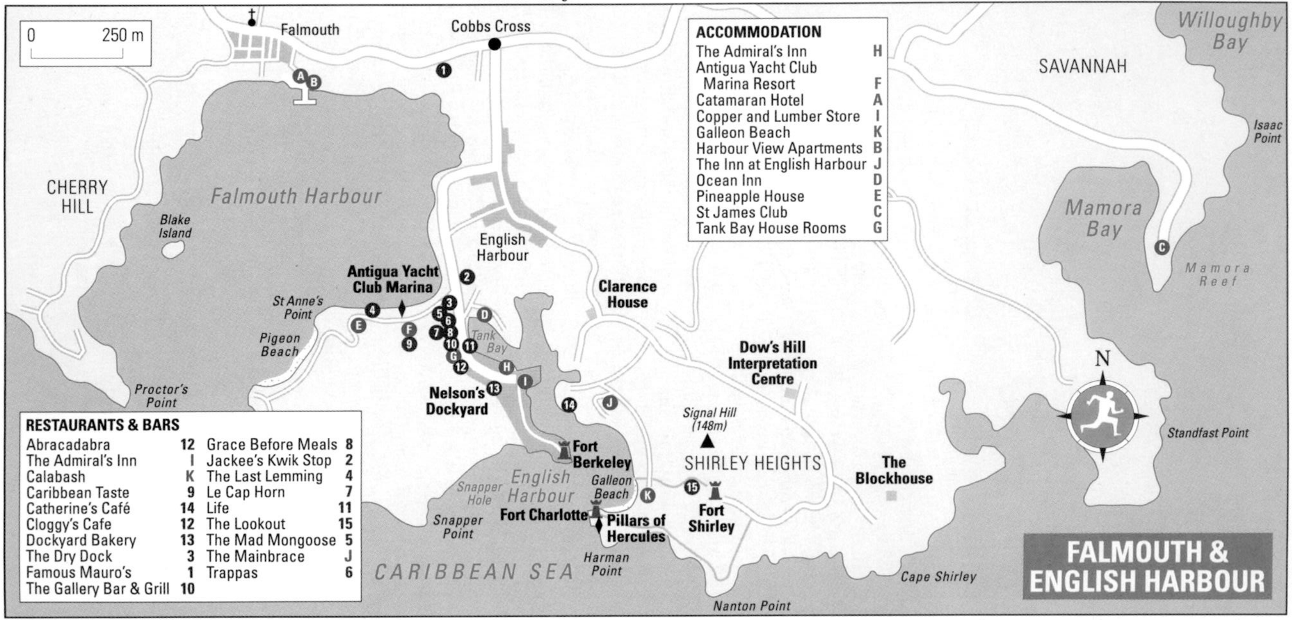

FALMOUTH & ENGLISH HARBOUR

ACCOMMODATION

The Admiral's Inn	H
Antigua Yacht Club Marina Resort	F
Catamaran Hotel	A
Copper and Lumber Store	I
Galleon Beach	K
Harbour View Apartments	B
The Inn at English Harbour	J
Ocean Inn	D
Pineapple House	E
St James Club	C
Tank Bay House Rooms	G

RESTAURANTS & BARS

Abracadabra	12
The Admiral's Inn	I
Calabash	K
Caribbean Taste	4
Catherine's Café	7
Cloggy's Cafe	9
The Dry Dock	11
Famous Mauro's	1
The Gallery Bar & Grill	10
Grace Before Meals	8
Jackee's Kwik Stop	2
The Last Lemming	7
Le Cap Horn	9
Life	14
The Lookout	12
The Mad Mongoose	13
The Mainbrace	5
Trappas	J
Dockyard Bakery	15
	6
	3

Willoughby Bay
Isaac Point
Mamora Reef
Standfast Point
SAVANNAH
Mamora Bay
N
Fort George
Cobbs Cross
Cherry Hill
Falmouth
Falmouth Harbour
Blake Island
Proctor's Point
St Anne's Point
Pigeon Beach
Antigua Yacht Club Marina
English Harbour
Clarence House
Nelson's Dockyard
Tank Bay
Snapper Hole
Snapper Point
Fort Berkeley
Fort Charlotte
English Harbour
Galleon Beach
Harman Point
Pillars of Hercules
CARIBBEAN SEA
Dow's Hill Interpretation Centre
Signal Hill (148m)
SHIRLEY HEIGHTS
Fort Shirley
The Blockhouse
Cape Shirley
Nanton Point
0   250 m

another track winds up to the fort.

English Harbour

The road east from Falmouth leads to the tiny village of Cobbs Cross, where a right turn takes you down to the small village of English Harbour, which somewhat confusingly borders a busy part of Falmouth Harbour. In addition to a few local homes, there are number of funky restaurants, bars, shops, hotels and Nelson's Dockyard (see below), which is one of the main attractions on the island.

Antigua Yacht Club Marina

This little practical oasis is built on a dock jutting into Falmouth Harbour, but in the town of English Harbour. On it you'll find a small Internet café, an ice cream shop, a grocery and liquor store, ship supplies, gift shops and a pleasant bookstore upstairs, Lord Jim's Locker, where the shelves are stocked with locally written children's books, sailing and travel books and flags.

Nelson's Dockyard

Daily 8am–6pm. US$5 or EC$13. Entry fee also covers Shirley Heights (see p.79). Adjacent to a fine natural harbour, one of Antigua's highlights is the eighteenth-century Nelson's Dockyard, the only surviving Georgian dockyard in the world. Though construction began in 1743, most of the present buildings date from between 1785 and 1792. Many of these buildings – such as the atmospheric *Admiral's Inn* hotel; see p.83 for review – were built from the ballast of bricks and stones brought to the island by British trading ships, who sailed "empty" from home to load up with sugar and rum.

The place developed primarily as a careening station, where British ships were brought to have the barnacles scraped from their bottoms and generally be put back into shape. The dockyard provided a crucial function for the military, providing them with a local base to repair, water and supply the navy that patrolled the West Indies and protected Britain's prized colonies against enemy incursion. However, during the nineteenth century, the advent of steam-powered ships, which needed less attention, coincided with a decline in British interest in the region, and the dockyard

▲ GREAT FORT GEORGE

▲ NELSON'S DOCKYARD

fell into disuse, finally closing in 1889.

Over the next sixty years the various dockyard buildings took a battering from hurricanes and earthquakes, until the 1950s saw a major restoration project as the dockyard began hosting yachts from the burgeoning charter industry. In 1961 the dockyard was officially reopened as both a working harbour and a tourist attraction. It was only then that the area got the name "Nelson's Dockyard" – apparently, the Antigua tourist board decided that a famous title was needed to market the place, and so they named it after the heralded British admiral, who as a young man was posted here for three years. Ironically enough, Nelson didn't like the island at all: he referred to Antigua in his correspondence as "this infernal hole" and "a vile spot".

Nevertheless, today the dockyard is a delightful place to wander around with plenty of places to eat, drink and shop. To get here, follow the main road south from English Harbour, which ends at a parking area. From there, the entrance to the dockyard takes you past the local post office, a bank and a small covered market, where vendors compete languidly for customers to buy their T-shirts and other souvenirs. If you plan to do any hiking in the area, ask for the free *Guide to the Hiking Trails in the National Parks* at the entrance gate. The same map and trail info is also available on the Antigua Museum website (Ⓦwww.antiguamuseums.org).

The Admiral's Inn

Nelson's Dockyard. Beyond the dockyard's mini-commercial zone, the first building on your left is *The Admiral's Inn*, built in 1788 and originally used as a store for pitch, lead and turpentine, with offices for the dockyard's engineers upstairs. Today it operates as a hotel and restaurant (see reviews, pp.83 & 85), yet it retains the original feel of the place, leaving an appealing atmosphere redolent of the dockyard's long history. Adjoining the hotel, a dozen thick, capped stone pillars – looking like the relics of an ancient Greek temple – are all that remain of a large boathouse, where ships used to be pulled in

Sailing Week

Begun in 1967 with a tiny fleet of wooden fishing boats, and now regularly graced by over 200 quality yachts, the English Harbour Race is the centrepiece of Antigua's **Sailing Week**, a festival of racing and partying that transforms the area around Nelson's Dockyard into a colourful, crowded carnival village and the harbour into a parking area for every type of sailing boat. Don't expect to find a lot of Antiguans present – it's predominantly a party for the American and European sailing contingent – but if you're on the island in late April/early May it's a good place to see some superb sailing action and squeeze in a heavy night of bar-hopping. For more information check ⓦwww.sailingweek.com.

along a narrow channel to have their sails repaired in the sail-loft on the upper floor.

The Dockyard Museum

Nelson's Dockyard. Daily 8am–6pm.
Down a lane from *The Admiral's Inn*, just beyond various restored colonial buildings and a 200-year-old sandbox tree, you'll come to the Admiral's House, a local residence (never actually used by an admiral) which was built in 1855 and today serves as the dockyard's museum.

The museum is worth a quick tour for its small but diverse collection that focuses on the dockyard's history and on Antigua's shipping tradition, with models and photographs of old schooners and warships. Also look out for the cups and records celebrating the various races held during the annual Sailing Week, when English Harbour almost disappears under a tide of visiting yachts and their crews (see box above). Finally, right across the street from the museum is Dockyard Pottery, a little gift shop with locally made bags, crafts, books, photographs and prints.

Officers' quarters at Nelson's Dockyard

Just beyond the bougainvillea-festooned *Copper and Lumber Store*, which now serves as an elegant hotel and restaurant (see reviews, p.84), are the officers' quarters – one of the most striking buildings in the dockyard, with a graceful double staircase sweeping up to a long, arcaded veranda. Ships' officers lived here during the hurricane season, when most of the fleet docked in English Harbour for protection. The building sits on a huge water cistern of twelve separate tanks, with a capacity for 240,000 gallons of water, and today provides space for an art gallery, boutique, bar and other stores. The downstairs offices house the immigration and customs authorities.

Fort Berkeley

A stroll around the dramatic military ruins of Fort Berkeley should be an integral part of your visit to the area. Built onto a narrow spit of land that guards the entrance to English Harbour, the fort was the harbour's earliest defensive point and retains essentially the same shape today that it had in 1745.

To get there, take the narrow path that leads from behind the *Copper and Lumber Store* down to the water's edge; go around the small wooden dock, up some steps and onto the trail leading to the fort, ten minutes' walk out onto the headland. On your right, above the craggy, wave-swept rocks, cannons once lined most of the wall facing out to sea, with the main body of the fort at the far end of the walkway comprising sentry boxes, a recently restored guardhouse and a gunpowder magazine. An early nineteenth-century Scottish cannon still stands guard at the fort, and the place offers spectacular views out to sea and back across English Harbour and Galleon Beach. Across the entrance to the harbour you can just see the beginning of the Pillars of Hercules (see p.80).

The Middle Ground and Fort Cuyler

For some rather more strenuous hiking, about half way out to Fort Berkeley a trail on your right, marked with white paint dots, leads to the peninsula known as the Middle Ground, where more military ruins sprinkle the landscape. It's a stiff clamber to the top of the hill, where a circular base is all that remains of the one-gun Keane battery that stood here until the early nineteenth century. Still, standing up here you'll get a clear picture of the strategic importance of the Middle Ground for defending both Falmouth Harbour to the west and English Harbour to the east. Continue along this trail to the remains of Fort Cuyler, where more gun emplacements and crumbling barracks walls stand as further testament to the military domination of the area. You'll need all your tracking skills to keep to the paths around here as goats and the occasional goatherd are the only users of the old soldiers' tracks these days, and there is a fair amount of prickly cactus and thorn bush to contend with – but the hike offers spectacular views over the harbours, the ocean and the desert-like landscape of the Middle Ground. You can continue along the trail to end up at Pigeon Beach (see below). From here you can retrace your steps back to the dockyard, or walk along the road into English Harbour.

Pigeon Beach

A good place to head for a swim is Pigeon Beach, five minutes' drive or twenty minutes' walk west of the dockyard. As you head out, turn

▼ FORT BERKELEY, ENGLISH HARBOUR

▲ RUINS AT SHIRLEY HEIGHTS

left just before you reach Falmouth Harbour and follow the road past some restaurants and the Antigua Yacht Club. Take the road uphill, which turns to the left, and then take a sharp right down to the wide expanse of white sand. When the harbour is full of boats the beach can get a little crowded, but generally it's a lovely, secluded spot. There is an excellent local beach shack, *Bumpkins*, with simple inexpensive food and cold drinks.

Shirley Heights

US$5 or EC$13 from 9am to 5pm; otherwise free. Entry fee also covers Nelson's Dockyard (see p.75). Spread over an extensive area of the hills to the east of English Harbour, numerous ruined military buildings offer further evidence of the strategic importance of this part of southern Antigua. Collectively known as Shirley Heights (although technically this is only the name for the area around Fort Shirley), it's an interesting area to explore, with a couple of adventurous hiking opportunities for those who

want to escape the crowds completely.

The area is named after General Sir Thomas Shirley, who, as governor of the Leeward Islands, was based in Antigua from 1781 to 1791. At a time when British Caribbean possessions were fast falling to the French – Dominica in 1778, St Vincent and Grenada in 1779 – and with British forces in America surrendering in 1781, Shirley insisted on massive fortification of Antigua to protect the naval dockyard. Building continued steadily for the next decade and, although the threat diminished after the French were finally defeated in 1815, the military complex was manned until 1854. Since then, it has been steadily eroded by a succession of hurricanes and earthquakes.

Clarence House

Shirley Heights. Following the road uphill from English Harbour, you'll pass the entrance to the late eighteenth-century Clarence House, an attractive Georgian house built in 1787 for Prince William, Duke of Clarence (later King

William IV), who was then serving in the Royal Navy. At the time of writing, the place was closed pending renovations. However, upon completion, it will house a museum covering the lives of people who have stayed here, including the duke, various governors-general of Antigua and the Leeward Islands, and the late Princess Margaret and the Earl of Snowdon, who spent their honeymoon here in 1960.

Galleon Beach

Shirley Heights. Past Clarence House, a right-hand turn-off leads down to *The Inn at English Harbour* (see review, p.84), as well as the attractive crescent of Galleon Beach, where numerous yachts are normally anchored just offshore. You'll see a huge, old anchor planted on shore to which large sailing vessels of yesteryear once attached lines to pull, or "warp", themselves into the harbour. This is one of the better beaches on this part of the island; the calm, shallow waters are great for swimming.

Pillars of Hercules

Shirley Heights. These gigantic rock columns are a unique geologic phenomenon and have served as an aid to navigation, marking the entrance to English Harbour for hundreds of years. The rock is of volcanic origin, laid down in layers, broken apart by fractures and then eroded by the sea to form these spectacular columns almost twenty metres high. To hike to the Pillars, you should wear footwear that can get wet, especially if the tide is high, and be careful on the slippery rocks. Do not attempt the hike if the seas are rough, as surging waves could carry you away.

Start from the end of Galleon Beach. Just past the last cottage take the trail following the water up and over a little hill, down to a pleasant small beach. Continue along the coast, where you'll have to clamber over rocks, until you come to a point of land with some ruins overgrown by tamarind trees. Cut across this point toward the ocean, climb over a field of boulders and around the next corner you'll be at the base of

▼ GALLEON BEACH

the Pillars. Keep an eye on the ground for tropical rocky intertidal creatures such as nerite snails, chitons and crabs, and look in tide pools for small fish, urchins and corals. Explore further down the coast for some fun rock climbing – suitable for all levels of experience.

You can hire an Apple water taxi (around US$2 per person) at the Dockyard to bring you to the pleasant small beach to begin your hike to the Pillars, or alternatively have them take you out by boat just to see them.

Dow's Hill

Shirley Heights. ☎ 481 5045. Daily 9am–5pm. Free with admission to Shirley Heights. Past the turn-off down to Galleon Beach you'll come to the Shirley Heights admission booth; just past it, up on the right, sits the Dow's Hill Interpretation Centre. Outside the centre you'll find the scant remains of the Dow's Hill Fort and some lovely views of nearby forts that the museum staff will be happy to point out for you. Indoors there's a collection of local shells and an odd fifteen-minute "multimedia" exhibition, with an adult voice answering a child's questions about the country's history from the Amerindians to the present. This overly simplified version of Antiguan history can be interesting for kids, but otherwise you're not missing much if you skip it, especially if you're short on time.

Cape Shirley and the Blockhouse

Shirley Heights. Beyond the Interpretation Centre, the road runs along the top of a ridge before dividing where a large cannon has been upended in the centre of the road. Fork left for the cliff called Cape Shirley, where you'll find a collection of ruined stone buildings – including barracks, officers' quarters and an arms storeroom – known collectively as the Blockhouse. On the eastern side, a wide gun platform looks downhill to Indian Creek (see p.82) and beyond, to Standfast Point peninsula and Eric Clapton's enormous house, as well as out over the vast sweep of Willoughby Bay. Every year, stories leak out that Clapton and friends such as Elton John and Keith Richards have turned up to jam at one of the island's nightclubs – but don't count on seeing them.

Officers' quarters at Fort Shirley

Shirley Heights. If you take the right-hand fork at the half-buried cannon, the road will lead you up to the further ruins of Fort Shirley. On the right as you approach are the still grandly arcaded (though now roofless) officers' quarters, overgrown with grass and surrounded by a chain-link fence.

The military cemetery

Shirley Heights. Opposite from the officers' quarters, across a bare patch of ground, are the ruins of the military hospital and, in a small valley just below the surgeon's quarters, the military cemetery. Here you'll find barely legible tombstones, dating mostly from the 1850s; disease – particularly yellow fever – was prevalent at that time. There's also an obelisk commemorating the men of the Dorset regiment, English soldiers who died while serving in the West Indies during the 1840s.

▲ MAMORA BAY

The Carpenter Rock Trail

Shirley Heights. Just uphill from the cemetery is a short red dirt road that ends at a precipice with a fantastic view down a dizzying sheer drop of over one hundred metres to the Atlantic Ocean. This is where the Carpenter Rock Trail ends or begins; look for the white painted dots on the rocks. Note that this trail makes for an excellent hike between Shirley Heights and English Harbour, the directions for which can be found in the free *Guide to Hiking Trails* available at the dockyard entrance.

The Lookout

Shirley Heights. The road from English Harbour ends at Fort Shirley itself, where a restored guardhouse now serves as an excellent little bar and restaurant (see reviews, pp.87 & 89). Beyond the guardhouse, the courtyard of the Lookout – where once a battery of cannons pointed out across the sea – now sees a battery of cameras snapping up the fabulous views over English Harbour, particularly on Sundays (and to a lesser extent Thursdays) when the tourists and Antiguans descend in droves for the reggae and steel bands. Visit on any other night for a quite peaceful sunset.

Indian Creek

From the Blockhouse (see p.81) it's a short but steep downhill hike to the bluff that overlooks Indian Creek, where, scattered along the shoreline, some of the island's most important Amerindian finds have been made. The hike passes down through scrubby grassland tended by goats and strewn with cacti, including the sometimes phallic red and green Turk's head cacti. At the bottom of the hill there's a small, sheltered but rocky beach, not great for swimming. The path continues up through a wood of cracked acacia trees and onto the deserted bluff, which offers grand views over the creek and, further east, to Mamora and Willoughby bays.

Mamora and Willoughby bays

From Cobbs Cross, avoiding the right turn to English Harbour, the road runs east towards a couple of quiet bays, namely tiny Mamora and the huge curve of Willoughby. It's an attractive drive, though there is little specific to see; Mamora Bay is dominated by the exclusive *St James Club* (see review on p.85) while the road past Willoughby Bay winds up through fields towards the old Betty's Hope sugar plantation (see p.64) and the island's east coast. Unless you're staying at *St James*, Mamora Bay is pretty difficult to visit. Easier to reach is Willoughby Bay, though its few beaches are unremarkable.

Liberta

Liberta was one of the first "free villages" established for emancipated slaves after Britain abolished slavery in 1807 and subsequently passed the Act of Emancipation in 1834. Today, even though Liberta is one of the largest settlements on the island, you'll find little reason to stop off and explore. On the main road through town, though, take note of two very striking churches: one of these, the pretty, pink church of Our Lady of Perpetual Help, is just by the turn-off to Fig Tree Drive (see p.90), while the other is a little further south, an unusual-looking affair in local green volcanic rock and red brick, with a red corrugated-iron roof and lovely stained-glass windows.

Swetes

Northwest of Liberta, Swetes is best known as the birthplace of cricketer Curtly Ambrose, the West Indies' leading fast bowler during the 1990s, and of present-day local cricketing hero Ridley Jacobs (see p.42 for more on the Antiguan passion for cricket). There's not much in the way of sightseeing here, apart from a surprisingly well-preserved sugar mill.

Accommodation

The Admiral's Inn

Nelson's Dockyard ☎ 460 1153, ☏ 460 1534, ⊛ www.admiralsantigua .com. Built in 1788 as the dockyard's supply store and now attractively restored, this classy inn is one of the most romantic accommodation options on Antigua, with welcoming staff and decent prices. The lovely old rooms, most with four-poster beds, run from US$140/90 in winter/summer. An occasional free boat ferries guests to a nearby beach.

Antigua Yacht Club Marina Resort

English Harbour ☎ 562 3030, ☏ 562 3031, ⊛ www.aycmarina.com. This large new resort is perched on the side of a steep hill overlooking Falmouth Harbour and the marina. You can stay in studio units with an ample bathroom and small balcony or larger suites with kitchens. The minimalist Asian-Italian furnishings are calming, if a bit sterile. There is no pool, but the beach is just a ten-minute walk away. Prices start at US$250/180 winter/summer.

Catamaran Hotel

Falmouth ☎ 460 1036, ☏ 460 1339, ⊛ www.catamaran-antigua.com. Friendly, relaxing place on the north side of the harbour in Falmouth, adjacent to a small marina. Enjoy sweeping harbour views, a nice little beach, a pool and comfortable rooms – some with kitchenettes – starting at US$130/105 in winter/summer. The owner is building a casual waterfront eatery right next door.

The Copper and Lumber Store

Nelson's Dockyard ☎ 460 1058, ⓕ 460 1529, ⓦ www.copperandlumberhotel.com. Elegant Georgian hotel in the heart of the dockyard, used from the late eighteenth century as its name suggests, with a dozen superb rooms (US$325/275 in winter/summer), some fabulously furnished with mostly nautically themed antiques. Quiet at night, but a short walk from a handful of good restaurants and nightlife.

Galleon Beach

Freeman's Bay ☎ 460 1024, ⓕ 460 1450, ⓦ www.galleonbeach.com. Pleasant little spot on a fine beach at the entrance to English Harbour offering decent but unremarkable cottages and villas, some in the garden and some on the beach. Prices start at US$225/140 winter/summer.

Harbour View Apartments

Falmouth ☎ 460 1762, ⓕ 463 6375, ⓦ www.antigua-apartments.com. Modern block with a small pool and six self-catering apartments, all overlooking the harbour, by a small and unexceptional beach. Good option for a family on a budget, as rooms sleep up to four and cost $190/140 a night in winter/summer.

The Inn at English Harbour

English Harbour ☎ 460 1014, ⓕ 460 1603, ⓦ www.theinn.ag. Attractive old hotel, popular with repeat guests and spread over a large site beside the harbour, next to a pleasant white-sand beach. There are 24 elegant suites bedecked in bougainvillea, and ten individual cottages. Prices start at US$222/178 in winter/summer.

Ocean Inn

English Harbour ☎ 463 7950, ⓕ 460 1263, ⓦ www.theoceaninn.com. Small, friendly inn perched on a hillside above English Harbour, with six doubles and four cottages starting at US$75/55 a night in high/low season for a room with shared bath or US$150/85 for double cottages with private bath. There's a tiny pool, spectacular views over Nelson's Dockyard and plenty of peace and quiet even though it's just a few minutes' walk from all the action.

▲ ADMIRAL'S INN

Pineapple House

English Harbour ☏ 560 3116, 🖰 www
.pineapplehouseantigua.com.
This is the closest you'll find to
a hostel in Antigua – and it sits
amid a garden hillside with
views of Falmouth Harbour.
Individual canopied beds
(US$45–65) are scattered
throughout the main house and
on open-air verandas. There are
also a few private cottages
(US$80–150). You'll find a help-
yourself cocktail bar and a
communal kitchen, which
makes for an open social setting
for visiting yachtsmen and
travellers. The whole place has
the vibe of a group of folks
crashing at a friend's Caribbean
pad for a long weekend. While
not for everyone, those looking
for a cheap, informal digs are in
the right spot.

St James Club

Mamora Bay ☏ 460 5000, 🖷 460 3015,
🖰 www.stjamesclubantigua.com.
On a peninsula surrounded by
the sea on three sides, this fine
resort offers rooms, suites and
villas, all with a sea view. It's
often busy with a largely British
clientele. You'll find four
restaurants (plus room service),
four bars, a small casino, two
beaches, six tennis courts and
four swimming pools on the
100-plus acres. There are plenty
of complimentary water sports
and an on-site dive shop
offering dives and certification.
Rates start at US$475/570 low/
high season all-inclusive or
US$265/350 on the European
plan (without meals).

Tank Bay House Rooms

English Harbour ☏ 561 0845,
🖂 marilynlinnington@hotmail.com.
The newly built Anchorage
Centre consists of a small open
courtyard ringed with a few
restaurants and business offices.
They also have five small, basic,
clean rooms (US$65/50) with
fans and private baths.

Restaurants and bars

Abracadabra

English Harbour ☏ 460 1732 or 460
2701, 🖷 463 8084, 🖰 www
.theabracadabra.com. Daily 10am–4pm
and 7–11pm. Closed Jun, Jul, Sept and
Oct. Just outside the dockyard,
the cosy *Abracadabra* offers a
mostly Southern Italian menu of
pastas, grilled meat and fish
(EC$30–60). Enjoy live jazz on
Mondays and a DJ or other live
music several nights a week (see
p.88).

The Admiral's Inn

Nelson's Dockyard ☏ 460 1027. Daily
7am–9.30pm. Good, unpretentious
dining in the old *Admiral's Inn*
building or, more romantically,
by the water's edge, with
occasional local dishes such as
Creole conch among the more
standard meals of fish, chicken
and salads (EC$25–40). Saturday
nights a mellow steel band plays
outdoors for diners.

Bumpkins

Pigeon Beach ☏ 562 2522. Daily
11.30am–8pm. Relaxing little
beach bar and restaurant with
Caribbean music, cold beer and
frozen drinks, and tasty
inexpensive eats like burgers,
jerk chicken and fish for
EC$16–35.

Calabash

Galleon Beach ☏ 460 1452. Daily for
lunch and dinner. Airy terrace
restaurant close to the beautiful
Galleon Beach (see opposite).
Savoury salads at lunch for

PLACES

Falmouth and English Harbour

▲ THE LAST LEMMING

EC$30–40 and a "world food tour" for dinner with mains such as grilled Cajun-style mahi mahi, Thai curry, grilled steak, teriyaki salmon and Caribbean seafood stew ranging from EC$35–75.

Caribbean Taste
Behind *Grace Before Meals*, English Harbour ☎ 562 3049. Daily for breakfast, lunch and dinner. Flavourful Antiguan fare in this small restaurant tucked away among local residences just before the entrance to the dockyard. Servings include large portions of ducana and salt cod, fungi and conch stew, curried goat, jerk chicken and various kinds of rotis, all for around EC$12–35. Wash it down with delicious fruit juices like soursop, guava and passion fruit.

Catherine's Café
Antigua Slipway, across from Nelson's Dockyard, English Harbour ☎ 460 5050. Wed–Mon for lunch and dinner, closed mid-May to mid-July. Tuck into tasty fare and take in the wonderful views at this laid-back French café on a shaded terrace by the water's edge. The simple but imaginative menu includes clams, oysters, *moules*

marinières and Sambuca prawns at EC$40–65 as well as some spectacular desserts, such as *tarte tatin*. You have to take a water taxi from the dockyard to get here or, if you've got a car, head in the direction of Shirley Heights and turn down the Antigua Slipway road.

Cloggy's
English Harbour ☎ 460 1732 or 460 2701. Mon–Sat for breakfast and lunch. Sharing the same building as *Abracadabra* (see p.85), this hip and casual spot serves tasty, healthy fruit smoothies, salads and baguette sandwiches (EC$22–45). You can also order international newspapers here.

Dockyard Bakery
Nelson's Dockyard ☎ 460 1474. Daily 7.30am–4pm. Pleasant place for breakfast or daytime snacks. Try the guava danishes, pineapple turnovers and bread pudding (EC$3), all freshly baked in the dockyard's old kitchens.

Famous Mauro's
Cobbs Cross ☎ 460 1318. Open most nights. One of the best places for pizza on Antigua, with more than thirty types available at night (EC$20–35), all freshly

cooked in the wood-burning oven. During the day they sell fresh croissants and breads from a window.

The Gallery Bar and Grill

English Harbour ☎ 562 5678. Wed–Mon for dinner. International grill serving fresh seafood and meats. Popular dishes include seafood gumbo (EC$40) and crispy duck (EC$45) and an array of tapas (EC$15–25). They have tables inside and out, a large bar and European house music.

Grace Before Meals

English Harbour ☎ 460 1298. Mon–Sat lunch and dinner. Basic, no-frills eatery with good local foods and fruit juices. Regular dishes include roti, stew fish, stew beef and curry chicken for EC$12–20.

Jackee's Kwik Stop

Falmouth Harbour ☎ 460 1299. Mon–Sat for breakfast and lunch. One of the best of the local eateries run by the delightful Jackee, this little café sells basic burgers and sandwiches as well as a few Antiguan specialities like roti and stew beef for EC$10–30. Their big breakfasts include the meat lover's special for EC$19.

The Last Lemming

Falmouth Harbour ☎ 460 6910. Daily for lunch and dinner. Closed June & July. Good food at this frequently crowded harbourside spot, including salads and sandwiches (EC$25–45), and seafood, chicken and steaks (EC$40–75). They also have a nice Sunday brunch for EC$24–40. Local bands play on Tuesdays and Fridays.

Le Cap Horn

Between Falmouth and English Harbour ☎ 460 1194. Mon–Sat 6.30–11pm. Closed May–Oct. French-Peruvian chef Gustavo prepares specialities from different regions of France using local meats and fish (EC$50–70), while his wife Helene does the desserts in this mellow garden restaurant. There's also an excellent pizzeria with a wood-burning brick oven (pizzas EC$28–40).

Life

English Harbour ☎ 562 2353 or 723 3502, ⓔ lifebarantigua@yahoo.com. Tues–Fri and Sun for lunch and dinner. Closed Sept. This lively bar and restaurant sits over the water on a pier just outside the dockyard. Aphorisms on "life" are painted everywhere and it's colourfully lit and particularly festive at night. Lunch fare of fish and chips or burgers are overpriced, but the dinner menu of grilled fish and steaks, bangers and mash and various curries is a good deal at EC$35; there's also a tasty kids' menu for EC$20.

The Lookout

Shirley Heights ☎ 460 1785. Mon–Thurs 9am–8pm, Fri–Sun 9am–10pm. The only place for a refreshment break while you're up on Shirley Heights, with a large patio providing superb views over the harbour and the dockyard. Simple meals such as BBQ chicken and shrimp and steak are EC$20–60. Their famous Sunday night barbecues pull a huge crowd for the reggae and steel band that play from early afternoon through to the late evening. On Thursday afternoons, the seven-piece Halcyon Steel Orchestra plays to a smaller crowd.

The Mad Mongoose

Falmouth Harbour ☎ 4637900. Bar 1pm–late; dinner served 6.30–10pm. Right in the heart of the action

▲ THE LOOKOUT

at English Harbour, this often lively bar – which gets absolutely packed when the boats are in – serves snacks and simple meals like sandwiches and burgers (EC$15–25) as well as steak and Guinness pie or fresh mahi mahi for EC$35. They also have a pool table and live reggae and soca on Friday nights.

The Mainbrace

At *The Copper and Lumber Store*, Nelson's Dockyard. Daily for breakfast, lunch and dinner. Closed summers. Good breakfasts for around US$14 at this Georgian inn; typical English pub lunches – burgers, chillies, etc – at around US$20; and in the evenings, more formal and more costly dining (entrées such as grilled steak and fish from US$25) in *The Copper and Lumber Store*'s stylishly renovated wardroom.

Trappas

English Harbour ☎ 562 3534. Tues–Sat 6.30–10pm. Locals and visitors pack this casual place nightly, feasting on delicious and reasonably priced fare like starters of fresh salads, hummus, mussels and nachos (all for EC$20) and mains of Thai curries, chicken or beef fajitas and blackened mahi mahi (EC$40).

Entertainment and nightlife

Abracadabra

English Harbour ☎ 460 1732 or 460 2701, ☎ 463 8084, ⊛ www. theabracadabra.com. Nightly 7pm until late. Closed Jun, Jul, Sept and Oct. No cover. Once dinner is over, the lights dim and *Abracadabra* often becomes a hopping nightspot: DJs from the US and Europe spin the latest house music, and live bands get everyone up for some open-air dancing on a small dance floor next to the restaurant (see p.85). They also feature costume parties, while the chill-out garden out back has mellower music and hammocks.

The Dry Dock

Falmouth Harbour ☎ 460 3040. Basic sports bar serving simple food and drawing a crowd when big sporting or sailing events are projected on their large-screen TV. They also show movies once a week.

The Last Lemming

Falmouth Harbour ☎ 460 6910. Open nightly until late. No cover. Lively bar, particularly when the boats are in – it's right under the Antigua Yacht Club, with great views across the harbour. Often open later than anywhere else and featuring local bands on Tuesday and occasionally other nights.

Life

English Harbour ☎ 562 2353 or 723 3502, ✆ lifebarantigua@yahoo.com Tues–Fri and Sun. Closed Sept. In the evenings, this bar and restaurant (see p.87) often becomes a vibrant party scene, playing Sixties and Seventies music in counterpoint to the more modern sounds coming from across the street at *Abracadabra*.

Popular with both the sailing crowd and locals.

The Lookout

Shirley Heights ☎ 460 1785. Thurs 4–8pm & Sun 4–10pm. No cover. On Sunday afternoons steel pan and reggae bands set up on the Heights overlooking English Harbour for this legendary weekly party. There's a bar with a great rum punch, barbecued food, vendors selling trinkets and a fun party atmosphere, though at the peak of the season you'll find little room to move. Thursdays are less crowded and only the steel bands plays.

The Rasta Shack

English Harbour. Nightly 5pm–6am. Low-key, friendly bar with a small patio, good music and cold beer that gets busy late at night with the after-hours crowd.

The west coast

Tourism makes a firm impression on Antigua's west coast, with hotels dotted at regular intervals between the little fishing village of Old Road in the south and the capital, St John's, in the north. Two features dominate the area: a series of lovely beaches, with Darkwood probably the best of the bunch for swimming, snorkelling and beachcombing, and, in the southwest, a glowering range of hills known as the Shekerley Mountains, offering the chance for a hike and some panoramic views.

On the edge of the Shekerley range, the lush and thickly wooded Fig Tree Hill is as scenic a spot as you'll find. You can trek a number of good trails in this area. Some lead inland, to sites usually overlooked by tourists such as Boggy Peak and Green Castle Hill, while one, the forested Rendezvous Trail, leads east to Rendezvous Bay. Due west of St John's, the Five Islands peninsula has several hotels, some good beaches and the mighty ruins of the eighteenth-century Fort Barrington.

Fig Tree Drive

This scenic road runs west from Swetes (see p.83) through the most densely forested part of the island, Fig Tree Hill. You won't actually see any fig trees – the road is lined with bananas (known locally as figs), mango trees and coconut palms as it carves its way through mountains and tropical vegetation down to the south coast at Old Road (see p.92). About halfway along the drive, you'll pass a small roadside shack called the Culture Shop, where you can get a refreshing drink or fresh fruit as well as locally made jams, hot sauces and crafts.

▼ FIG TREE DRIVE

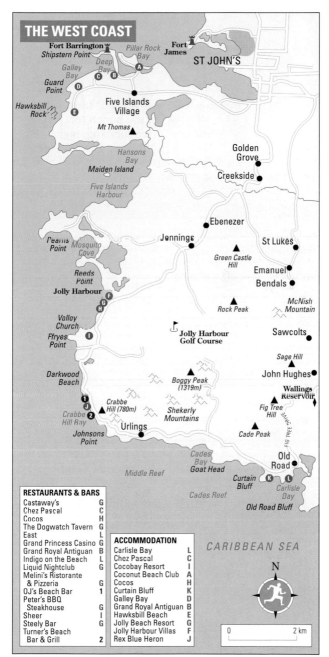

THE WEST COAST

Fort Barrington
Shipstern Point
Pillar Rock Bay
Fort James
ST JOHN'S
Galley Bay
Deep Bay
Guard Point
Hawksbill Rock
Five Islands Village
Mt Thomas
Golden Grove
Creekside
Hansons Bay
Maiden Island
Five Islands Harbour
Ebenezer
Jennings
St Lukes
Pearns Point
Mosquito Cove
Green Castle Hill
Emanuel
Bendals
Reeds Point
Jolly Harbour
McNish Mountain
Rock Peak
Valley Church
Ffryes Point
Jolly Harbour Golf Course
Sawcolts
Sage Hill
John Hughes
Darkwood Beach
Boggy Peak (1319m)
Wallings Reservoir
Crabbe Hill (780m)
Shekerly Mountains
Fig Tree Hill
Cade Peak
FIG TREE DRIVE
Crabbe Hill Bay
Urlings
Johnsons Point
Cades Bay
Goat Head
Old Road
Middle Reef
Curtain Bluff
Carlisle Bay
Cades Reef
Old Road Bluff

RESTAURANTS & BARS

Castaway's	G
Chez Pascal	C
Cocos	H
The Dogwatch Tavern	G
East	L
Grand Princess Casino	G
Grand Royal Antiguan	B
Indigo on the Beach	L
Liquid Nightclub	G
Melini's Ristorante & Pizzeria	G
OJ's Beach Bar	1
Peter's BBQ Steakhouse	G
Sheer	I
Steely Bar	G
Turner's Beach Bar & Grill	2

ACCOMMODATION

Carlisle Bay	L
Chez Pascal	C
Cocobay Resort	I
Coconut Beach Club	A
Cocos	H
Curtain Bluff	K
Galley Bay	D
Grand Royal Antiguan	B
Hawksbill Beach	E
Jolly Beach Resort	G
Jolly Harbour Villas	F
Rex Blue Heron	J

CARIBBEAN SEA

N

0   2 km

▲ SOUTHWEST ROAD, NEAR URLINGS

Rendezvous Trail

Next to the Culture Shop on Fig Tree Drive, a dirt road leads uphill to the Wallings Reservoir – the island's first – where you'll find picnic tables set up around the edge of the water. Serious hikers can take the Rendezvous Trail, which starts on your left just before you reach the steps of the reservoir. It crosses the Wallings Woodlands to the beautiful and usually empty beach a two-hour walk away at Rendezvous Bay (see p.72).

Even a fifteen-minute stroll repays the effort: the woodlands are the best remaining example of the evergreen secondary forest that covered the island before British settlers arrived. With numerous species of shrubs and trees, including giant mahogany trees (look for the carpets of asymmetrical pointed leaves on the ground), masses of noisy bird life and higher humidity, this is the closest you'll find to a rainforest in Antigua. Bear in mind, though, that while it's pretty hard to get lost, the main path is little used and in places can quickly become overgrown and hard to make out.

Old Road and Carlisle Bay

Once an important port and town, Old Road derived its name from nearby Carlisle Bay – a safe anchorage or "road" for the early settlers – but was soon surpassed by the new "roads" of St John's and Falmouth Harbour. Today Old Road is a small and rather impoverished fishing village, notably contrasted by the five-star *Carlisle Bay* hotel and the swanky *Curtain Bluff* resort (see pp.95 & 96). There is a superb swath of beach between the two that is open to the public.

Many locals have recently become passionate supporters of the English football club Liverpool and its star striker Emile Heskey; his father was born and lived in Old Road before moving to England in the 1960s.

Boggy Peak

Heading west from Old Road, the road follows the coast around Cades Bay, offering delightful views out to sea over

Cades Reef. On the right, about a kilometre from Old Road, a dirt road, just after a small banana farm and before the Cades Bay Pineapple Station, leads up into the Shekerley Mountains to Boggy Peak, which, at 400 metres, is the highest point on the island. The panoramic view from the top – in good visibility you can see St Kitts, Guadeloupe and Montserrat – is well worth the steep drive (4WD only) or one-hour climb. Unfortunately, the peak is now occupied by a communications station, safely tucked away behind a high-security fence, so you'll need to make arrangements to visit with Cable & Wireless in St John's (☎480 4000). If you haven't the time or the inclination, the views from outside the perimeter fence are almost as good. Winston Hazzard (☎461 8195) offers nature hikes to Boggy Peak or Wallings Woodlands for about US$20 per person with a minimum of four people.

Turner's, Darkwood and Coco beaches

Continuing west through the village of Urlings, the road runs alongside a number of excellent beaches. First up is Turner's Beach and Johnson's Point, where the sand shelves down to the sea beside a couple of good beach bars, including *Turner's* (see review, p.100), where you can also rent snorkelling gear.

The snorkelling is better just north of here at Darkwood Beach, a great spot to stop and take a swim, with a wide stretch of beach running right along the main road. Look out for small underwater canyons just offshore, and schools of squid and colourful reef fish. Beachcombers will find this one of the best places on the island to look for shells and driftwood. There are a couple of groves of Casuarina trees for shade, as well as *OJ's*, another friendly little beach bar that offers excellent and inexpensive food (see p.79).

Lastly, Coco Beach is reached via a turn-off signposted to the *Cocobay Resort* (see p.95); follow the track for 500 metres past some old sugar mills for another magnificent stretch of sand, again strewn with driftwood and edged by a turquoise sea.

Jolly Harbour

Day passes for *Jolly Beach Resort* US$98 (full day), US$49 (half day).

Covering an immense area (much of it filled with wetlands) north of Coco Beach, the 450-room all-inclusive *Jolly Beach Resort* (see p.97) sprawls alongside a mile of one of Antigua's best beaches, with clear blue water lapping against the sugary white sand. A day pass for the beach, available from the resort, includes lunch, drinks and use of the watersports equipment; however it's free to use just the beach. Adjacent, the Jolly

▲ DARKWOOD BEACH

Harbour complex has a marina, rental apartments, a casino, restaurants and a small shopping mall. It's a world apart from the "real" Antigua – like a small piece of America transplanted in the Caribbean.

Green Castle Hill

If you haven't climbed Boggy Peak (see p.92) or Monk's Hill (aka, Great Fort George; see p.72), you could consider getting your panoramic view of Antigua from the top of Green Castle Hill. The peak is littered with natural formations of stone pillars and large rocks, which some believe are Stone Age megaliths left by Antigua's oldest inhabitants. The claim is patently absurd – there is no evidence of Antigua's Amerindians having either the technology or the inclination to erect such monuments to their deities – but don't let that put you off visiting. The views are superb, particularly to the north beyond St John's, and besides the odd goat, you won't see a soul around.

You'll really need a car to get here. Head inland from the main road between Jennings and St John's towards Emanuel; the path to the top (a forty-minute walk) begins by the gates of a small brick factory connected to a large stone quarry.

Five Islands peninsula

To the west of St John's the highway leads out through a narrow isthmus onto the large Five Islands peninsula, named after five small rocks that jut from the sea just offshore. There are several hotels on the peninsula, and some great beaches scattered about, but the interior is largely barren and scrubby, and there's not a lot to see.

Hawksbill Bay

To reach Hawksbill Bay and some excellent beaches, follow the main road straight through Five Islands peninsula, ignoring the turn-offs for the *Coconut Beach Club* and *Chez Pascal* (see opposite). Just before the *Hawksbill Beach Hotel*, you'll see a place to park and access to this fine stretch of beach. A kilometre offshore from the bay, a large rock in the shape of the head of a hawksbill turtle gives the place its name.

Fort Barrington and Deep Bay

On Goat Hill, at the northern point of Five Islands peninsula. Close to the *Grand Royal Antiguan* hotel (see p.96), the circular stone ruins of Fort Barrington overlook the gorgeous Deep Bay. The British first built a simple fort here in the 1650s, to protect the southern entrance to St John's Harbour, though it was captured by the French when they took the city in 1666. In 1779, at a time of renewed tension between the two nations, Admiral Barrington of the British navy enlarged and strengthened the fort. This time, the deterrent proved effective; like most of Antigua's defences, Fort Barrington never saw any further action, and spent the next two centuries as a signal station reporting on the movement of ships in the local waters.

Today, it's well worth the ten-minute hike up the steep hill to the fort. Once arrived, you'll be treated to a dramatic sense of isolation as you look out to sea or back over the tourists sunning themselves far below on the bay. To get there, take the right just before the entrance to the *Grand Royal Antiguan*. At the

▲ KAYAKING AT FIVE ISLANDS

end of the road, park your car, walk over a small metal bridge, and then find the trail up to the fort. Beware of the poisonous, overgrown Manchineel trees at the beginning of the trail and even at the fort itself. When you get down have a dip at the lovely calm beach near the large hotel.

Accommodation

Carlisle Bay

Old Road ☎ 484 0000, ℱ 484 0001, ⓦ www.carlisle-bay.com. "Barefoot luxury" – ie, luxury in a beach setting – is the overriding theme at this new resort. At a starting price of US$1000/750 a night winter/summer for a room with breakfast and afternoon tea, it's clearly not for everyone. But, it's beautifully designed – in low-key whites and greys with polished dark-wood furniture – and set in a fabulous location. The 88 suites face a peaceful white-sand beach with the dense forests of Fig Tree Hill all around. There's a gym, a spa, pools, tennis courts, a 45-seat cinema, a thoughtfully constructed library and two excellent restaurants (*Indigo on the Beach* and *East*). The resort's calm, lovely beach affords a striking view of nearby Montserrat, which is usually belching smoke and steam.

Chez Pascal

Galley Bay Hill, Five Islands ☎ 462 3232, ⓦ www.chezpascalantigua.com. In addition to being a fantastic French restaurant (see p.98), *Chez Pascal*, set in tropical gardens on a hillside above Galley Bay, also has four luxurious guestrooms with hot tubs and great views. Bed-and-breakfast rates run US$225/175 in high/low season.

Cocobay Resort

Ffryes Beach ☎ 562 2400, ℱ 562 2424, ⓦ www.cocobayresort.com. Excellent all-inclusive right by the beach, with twenty brightly painted fan-cooled cottages (from US$340/280 in winter/summer) scattered above a turquoise bay and overlooking the Shekerley Hills. There's a beautiful pool and an aromatherapy/massage treatment room (for which you pay extra). The inclusive food is just so-so, but there is a top-notch restaurant called *Sheer* (see p.99), for which you also pay extra.

Coconut Beach Club

Deep Bay ☎ 462 2520, ⦿www
.coconutbeachclub.com. On a
decent beach, and pleasantly
landscaped, this welcoming little
resort has its own supply of
small sailboats, and offers nature
walks and the occasional bout of
entertainment – live bands and
the like. The rooms are a good
size, with balcony, waterview
and hammock, and most have a
full kitchen. Prices are US$170/
140 a night in winter/summer.

Cocos

Lignum Vitae Bay ☎ 460 2626, ⓕ 462
9707, ⦿www.cocoshotel.com.
Another all-inclusive "get-away-
from-it-all" spot, ideal for
couples. The nineteen rooms are
very simply done (no TV, no
phone and a mosquito net
rather than air-conditioning),
but each has beautiful views out
over the ocean and across the
broad crescent of Jolly Beach.
There's good food, too, on the
candlelit terrace below (see
review, p.98). Rooms are
US$170/125 in winter/summer.

Curtain Bluff

Old Road ☎ 462 8400, ⓕ 462 8409,
⦿www.curtainbluff.com. This
spectacular all-inclusive hotel,
with two pretty beaches, is built
on the craggy bluff that
overlooks Carlisle Bay and
Cades Reef. The spacious rooms
with wicker furniture all have a
balcony or garden patio with a
view of the ocean. Rates
include all meals and drinks,
tennis, scuba diving, sportfishing
and a host of other top-class
facilities. Rooms can sometimes
feel stacked upon one another
and seem a bit overpriced at
US$950/645 a night in winter/
summer.

Grand Royal Antiguan

Deep Bay ☎ 462 3733, ⓕ 462 3732.
⦿www.grandroyalantiguan.com.
At nine storeys, this massive,
colourfully painted yet ugly
place feels like a big-city
concrete business hotel
accidentally plonked down in
the middle of the Caribbean.
That said, the facilities are
excellent, particularly for tennis
and watersports, the 277 rooms
are comfortable and the beach
busy but pleasant. If you can get
a decent rate as part of a
package (look for something in
the neighbourhood of
US$240/206 a night in winter/

▼ VIEW OF GRAND ROYAL ANTIGUAN, DEEP BAY

summer) it's not a bad place to stay – if you can handle the big crowds, that is.

Galley Bay

Five Islands ☎ 462 0302, ⓕ 462 4551. Sprouting up between a bird-filled lagoon and a kilometre-long stretch of palm-fringed beach, this resort is perfect for a romantic retreat. The seventy rooms, which are mixed nearly evenly between individual thatched-roof, white-plaster cottages and wooden Bahamian-style bungalows, are equipped with bathrobes and private patios or balconies, while some feature private pools. A large lagoon-like pool, grass tennis courts, watersports and two fine restaurants round out the package. All-inclusive rates begin at around US$825/650 a night during high/low season.

Hawksbill Beach

Five Islands ☎ 462 0301, ⓕ 462 1515, ⓦ www.hawksbill.com. Attractive all-inclusive hotel that sprawls over a vast area on the Five Islands peninsula, overlooking the bay and the jagged rock that pokes from the sea, giving the place its name. Four beaches, dramatic views, lovely landscaped gardens, and an old sugar mill (that's been converted into a gift shop) all add to the varied atmosphere of this multi-faceted resort. You'll find a range of accommodations, from quiet beachfront cottages and club rooms to suites with balconies looking out towards Hawksbill Rock – prices start at US$300/265 in winter/summer. A day pass to use their beach and facilities is US$60 (full day) and US$40 (half day).

▲ JOLLY BEACH RESORT

Jolly Beach Resort

Lignum Vitae Bay ☎ 462 0061, ⓕ 562 2302, ⓦ www.jollybeachresort.com. Vast all-inclusive resort – 462 small and rather unattractive rooms scattered along half a kilometre of good white sand beach – with four restaurants, seven bars, tennis courts and free watersports, including windsurfing, waterskiing, small sailboats and paddle boats. In a place this size, you can't avoid feeling part of a big crowd (what with the plastic bracelet you must wear at all times) and the food can be hit or miss, but on the whole the place offers pretty decent value. All-inclusive rates per couple start at US$280/260 in winter/summer.

Jolly Harbour Villas

Jolly Harbour ☎ 462 6166, ⓦ www.jollyharbourantigua.com. Modern complex of about fifty waterfront villas, mostly two-bedroom with a full kitchen and a balcony overlooking the harbour. Plenty of American-style shops, restaurants and sports facilities nearby (including a golf course and a large, communal swimming pool) plus a casino and nightclub. The resort feels somewhat bland and unimaginative, and not very

Antiguan. Doubles start at US$140/120 in winter/summer.

Rex Blue Heron

Johnson's Point ☎ 462 8564, ℱ 462 8005, ⓦ www.rexresorts.com.
Medium-sized and very popular all-inclusive on one of the best west coast beaches with a small pool just a stone's throw from the sea. The 64 comfortable, brightly decorated rooms are nothing special and neither are the grounds. Mostly an older crowd stays here. All-inclusive rates start at US$350/300 in winter/summer.

Restaurants and bars

Castaways

Jolly Harbour ☎ 562 4445. Daily for breakfast, lunch and dinner. Good beach bar and bistro on a nice if crowded strip of sand. The menu is basic with garlic shrimp (EC$55), coconut curried chicken (EC$46) and lunches of sandwiches and salads from EC$20-30.

Chez Pascal

Galley Bay Hill, Five Islands ☎ 462 3232, ℱ 460 5730, ⓦ www .chezpascalantigua.com. Tues–Sat for lunch and dinner. Closed Sept. This classy French restaurant, on the Five Islands peninsula, with fine views out to sea, deservedly has one of the best culinary reputations on the island. It was built by owner and chef Pascal Milliat, whose passion for cooking is evident in his mouth-watering fare and masterful use of herbs. Dishes include starters of snails with basil butter (EC$31) and light and fluffy chicken liver mousse with thyme (EC$29); mains of pan-fried snapper with capers, lime and cream (EC$78) and lobster thermidor (EC$98); and amazing desserts (EC$24). To get here, take a right at the fork before the *Galley Bay* hotel (see p.97), take a right and then go right again up a steep hill. Reservations required.

Cocos

At the *Cocos* hotel, Lignum Vitae Bay ☎ 460 2626, ⓦ www.cocoshotel.com. Daily for breakfast, lunch and dinner.
One of the most romantic spots on the island, with a candlelit terrace overlooking a gorgeous west-coast bay. The food's tasty too, including pumpkin soup and fish fingers for EC$16–30, and main courses of kingfish with fruit salsa and seafood penne pasta for EC$42–45.

The Dogwatch Tavern

Jolly Harbour ☎ 462 6550. Restaurant open daily from 6–11pm. Bar open Mon–Fri 4pm–late, Sat & Sun 5pm–late. This English-style pub, decorated with flags, pennants and sailing regalia, sits in the mini-mall beside the marina.

▲ THE DOGWATCH TAVERN

There are tables indoors and out, pool tables and dartboards, and a reasonably priced menu with burgers for EC$17, hot dogs for EC$12, flying fish sandwiches for EC$20 and seared ahi tuna for EC$45.

East
Carlisle Bay ☎ 484 0000. Daily for dinner after 7pm. Upscale Asian fusion restaurant at the *Carlisle Bay Hotel*, with tasty starters, soups and salads (US$12–18) and creative mains of Asian pan-cooked meats and fish, phad Thai and curries for US$18–32.

Indigo on the Beach
Carlisle Bay ☎ 484 0000. Daily for breakfast, lunch and dinner. Lovely restaurant right on the beach at the *Carlisle Bay Hotel*, with a great view of nearby Montserrat and its steaming volcano. Serving top-quality dishes such as roasted mahi mahi (US$24), fettuccini, shrimp and basil (US$26) and gnocchi with artichokes and asparagus (US$18).

Melini's Ristorante and Pizzeria
Jolly Harbour ☎ 462 7695. Daily except Sat & Sun for breakfast, lunch and dinner. Sat & Sun dinner only. Casual open-air Italian eatery right by the marina. The standard menu has pizzas for EC$26–36, steaks for EC$68 and schnitzels for EC$45, while specials might be duck breast with mango pepper jelly and island greens at EC$45 or lemon pepper tilapia at EC$38.

OJ's Beach Bar
Crabbe Hill Beach ☎ 460 0184, ☎ 462 8651. Daily 10am–11pm. Simple beach bar and restaurant on the water's edge between Darkwood Beach and Turner's Beach. The

▲ INDIGO ON THE BEACH

food is excellent – sandwiches and burgers for EC$15–25 and a house speciality of spice-coated red snapper for EC$30 – and the setting is wonderful: sand under your feet, the place festooned with fishing nets and carved driftwood (the fruit of the owner's passion for beachcombing) and, on a clear day, a spot-on view of the neighbouring island of Montserrat. Live jazz or reggae on Friday and Saturday nights.

Peter's BBQ Steakhouse
Jolly Harbour ☎ 462 6026. Daily for breakfast, lunch and dinner. Meat-oriented barbecue restaurant among the shops by the marina, with reasonable if unspectacular offerings. There are daily lunch specials like barbecued chicken and chips or sandwiches for just EC$15; dinners of steaks, lamb or seafood kebabs with rice or veal in cream sauce for EC$40–75; and an open salad bar for EC$26.

Sheer

At the *Cocobay Resort*, Ffryes Beach ☏562 2400. Tues–Sat 7–10.30pm. Wonderfully imaginative and eclectic food at this beautiful cliff-side restaurant, with only twelve tables and just one sitting. The menu, which fuses Asian and South American flavours, includes starters of smoked goose, conch ceviche or carpaccio of lobster (EC$36–46), and mains of guava-jerked pork tenderloin or citrus-dusted scallops (EC$65–75). Save room for the outstanding desserts.

Steely Bar

Jolly Harbour ☏462 6260. Daily 8am–late. Food is served up all day at this lively spot overlooking the marina in the heart of the Jolly Harbour complex. A full English or American breakfast costs EC$23, while an extensive lunch menu features various salads (EC$19–27), and hot dogs and burgers (EC$20–25). Dinner options might include Jamaican black pepper shrimp (EC$45) or Cajun snapper with rice (EC$43). There's entertainment some nights as well (see "Nightlife", below).

Turner's Beach Bar & Grill

Johnson's Point ☏462 9133. Daily 8am–9pm. Delightful little restaurant on another of the best west coast beaches, near the *Rex Blue Heron*. It's unpretentious and mellow, with plastic furniture right on the sand. The evening menu (with most dishes costing between $US12 and $US20) includes goat curry, grilled red snapper, shrimp in pineapple and conch fritters. A half grilled lobster goes for US$39. During the day, you'll find the same menu, but even if you're not particularly hungry, it's a great place to retreat from the beach for a snack and a beer.

Entertainment and nightlife

Grand Princess Casino

Jolly Harbour ☏562 9900, ⊛www.grandprincessentertainment.com. Open daily noon–late. Monstrous development in the heart of the Jolly Harbour area, with a massive casino, three restaurants and sometimes featuring live bands, games or karaoke.

Liquid Nightclub

At the Grand Princess Casino, Jolly Harbour ☏562 9900. Fri–Mon 10pm–late. Cover EC$30. This new, nicely air-conditioned club draws a late-night party crowd. The music is a mix of Latin, disco, R&B, reggae and calypso, while the people getting down to it are a mix of young Antiguans and visitors to the island.

Grand Royal Antiguan

Five Islands ☏462 3733. Open nightly. No cover. Normally the liveliest spot on the Five Islands peninsula, this hotel (open to non-guests; see p.96) has a small disco and a casino area with pool tables, slots and video games.

Steely Bar

Jolly Harbour ☏462 6260. Open nightly until late, closed Sunday after 6pm. No cover charge. The main all-around entertainment centre for the Jolly Harbour area, with large TVs showing sports matches, a steel band on Tuesday nights, karaoke on Saturday and always a crowd of people milling about. See p.99 for a review of its kitchen.

Barbuda and Redonda

With its magnificent deserted beaches, spectacular coral reefs and large colony of frigate birds, the nation's other inhabited island, Barbuda – 48km to the north of Antigua – is well worth a visit. Don't expect the same facilities as on Antigua; accommodation options are limited, as are snorkelling and diving gear, and you'll find that schedules – whether for taxis, boats or meals – tend to drift. This is all, of course, very much part of the island's attraction.

Barbuda is a buzzing metropolis, however, compared with Antigua's other "dependency", the tiny and now uninhabited volcanic rock known as Redonda, some 56km to the southwest in the main chain of the Lesser Antilles, between Nevis and Montserrat.

Codrington

Codrington, Barbuda's capital and only settlement, holds almost the entire population of 1500 people within its grid of narrow streets. It's a well spread-out place, with plenty of brightly painted single-storey clapboard or concrete buildings. There is a bank (with an ATM), a small Internet café, a few guesthouses, a handful of restaurants, bars and grocery stores, but, for the most part there is little sign of life apart from a few teens listening to tunes on their cell phones and some old-timers on their porches watching folks pass by. On Sundays the capital livens up

▼ HORSES IN CODRINGTON

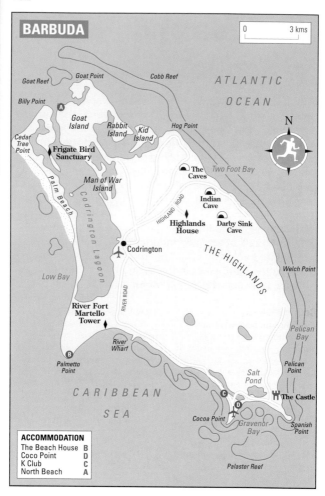

BARBUDA

0   3 kms

ATLANTIC

OCEAN

Goat Reef

Goat Point

Cobb Reef

Billy Point

Goat Island

Rabbit Island

Kid Island

Hog Point

Cedar Tree Point

Frigate Bird Sanctuary

Two Foot Bay

N

Palm Beach

Man of War Island

Codrington Lagoon

HIGHLAND ROAD

The Caves

Indian Cave

Darby Sink Cave

Highlands House

Codrington

THE HIGHLANDS

Welch Point

Low Bay

RIVER ROAD

River Fort Martello Tower

River Wharf

Pelican Bay

Pelican Point

Palmetto Point

Salt Pond

The Castle

CARIBBEAN

SEA

Cocoa Point

Gravenor Bay

Spanish Point

Palaster Reef

ACCOMMODATION

The Beach House	B
Coco Point	D
K Club	C
North Beach	A

with horse races at the local track, followed by crowds of young people milling about in Madison Square and dancing in bars like *The Lime* (see p.110).

Codrington Lagoon

To the west of town, Codrington Lagoon is an expansive area of exceptionally clear, hypersaline water, fringed by mangroves. The lagoon is completely enclosed on its western side by the narrow but magnificent strip of Palm Beach (see p.104), but there is a narrow cut to the north where fishing boats can get out to the ocean. Lobsters breed in the lagoon and you may see them at the pier being loaded for export to Antigua – an important contribution to the local economy.

▲ CODRINGTON LAGOON

Frigate bird sanctuary

To the northwest of Codrington Lagoon, a series of mangrove clumps known as Man of War Island serve as the home and breeding ground for the largest group of frigate birds anywhere in the Caribbean.

You'll need a boat to get anywhere near these birds, motoring out to the edge of the shallows where they live and then poling the boat punt-like to their nests. The sight as you approach is quite spectacular – the mothers will take to the skies as you draw near, joining the multitude of birds wheeling above you, and leaving their babies standing imperiously on the nest but watching you closely out of the corner of their eyes. The display gets even more dramatic during the mating season, from late August to December, when hundreds of the males put on a grand show – puffing up their bright-red throat pouches as they soar through the air just a few metres above the females, watching admiringly from the bushes.

Small boats leave for the Frigate bird sanctuary from the small pier in Codrington and charge around US$50 per boat, plus a US$2 per person fee for entrance to the sanctuary. If you just turn up without notice, you will likely find someone to take you out, but it's advisable to make arrangements through your hotel or at the airport's small tourist booth.

Highlands House

North of Codrington, a few dirt roads fan out across the upper part of Barbuda. The largest of them, Highland Road, leads northeast to the uplifted bit of land appropriately called the Highlands. Between some fields a small red dirt road on the right leads up to the scant remains of Highlands House, the castle the first Codringtons built on the island in the seventeenth century. The Codrington brothers, Christopher and John, were granted a lease on the island by King Charles II in 1685 in exchange for "one fat sheep yearly if demanded". They used the island to raise provisions (and more slaves) to support their vast sugar plantations in Antigua. Their home must have been pretty extensive, for the ruins – crumbling walls and the occasional piece of staircase

– cover a wide area. The views across the island from here are as panoramic as you'll find.

Indian Caves

Follow Highland Road until it ends and you'll find yourself at the foot of a series of caves that have been naturally carved into the low cliffs. These are thought to have sheltered Taino and possibly Carib Indians in the centuries preceding the arrival of Europeans. However, scant evidence of their presence has been found here, except for some unusual petroglyphs.

The entrance to the main cave is opposite a large boulder, with the ruins of an old watchtower built up alongside. You'll need to scramble up the rocks for five minutes, then make a short, stooped walk inside the cave to reach the petroglyphs – a couple of barely distinguishable and very amateurish faces carved into the rock face. What is more noticeable is where pieces of rock have been prised away, a decade or so ago, by tourist vandals eager for their own chunk of ancient art. Alongside the petroglyphs, a large dome-shaped chamber – the "presidential suite" – was

probably the main home of the Indians within the complex.

A couple of kilometres east of these caves, the Darby Sink Cave is one of hundreds of sinkholes on the island, dropping seventy feet to a mini-rainforest where palmetto palm trees, shrubs and birds proliferate. It's a steep climb down into the sinkhole, and a bit difficult to find, so you're probably best going with a local guide.

Beaches

Barbuda boasts some of the most spectacular deserted white- and pink-sand beaches in the Caribbean. At many places around the island you'll spot tiny bays and coves where you can jump out of your car for a private swim and some snorkelling.

On the west coast, on the far side of Codrington Lagoon (and so only really accessible by boat), gently curving **Palm Beach** offers 16km of dazzling white sand interspersed with long stretches of pink, created by the tiny fragments of millions of seashells washed up over the years. It's a great place to sunbathe, swim and snorkel,

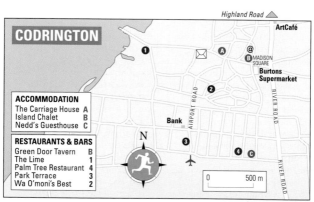

CODRINGTON

ArtCafé

@

MADISON SQUARE

Burtons Supermarket

ACCOMMODATION
The Carriage House   A
Island Chalet   B
Nedd's Guesthouse   C

RESTAURANTS & BARS
Green Door Tavern   B
The Lime   1
Palm Tree Restaurant   4
Park Terrace   3
Wa O'moni's Best   2

AIRPORT ROAD

RIVER ROAD

Bank

N

0   500 m

River Wharf

Getting there and getting around

The only scheduled **flights** to Barbuda are from Antigua on Carib Aviation (local ☎481 2400, UK ☎01895/450 710, ✉caribav@itgmarketing.co.uk). Two flights leave daily from the main airport in Antigua (7.45am and 5pm, returning thirty minutes later in each case) and cost US$74 round-trip. The flight takes twenty minutes and you must be at the airport one hour prior to your departure. The journey can also be made by **boat** aboard the speedy Barbuda Express Catamarans (☎764 2291 in Antigua or ☎460 0059 in Barbuda, ⊛www.antiguaferries.com). They depart once or twice every day except Tuesday, cost EC$140 round-trip and take about 90min. The ride out to Barbuda can be a bit choppy when the winds are blowing strong.

When you visit, **getting around** is something you'll need to plan out. There is no bus service, and distances (and the heat) are sufficient to put all but the hardiest off the idea of walking anywhere. Recently, there has been an increase in the number of **taxis**, and you can usually catch a ride anywhere in Codrington for EC$10 or between town and *The Beach House* for EC$30. A good way to explore the island is to **rent a 4WD** from a private citizen: try Lynton Thomas (☎721 2796), Byron Askie (☎460 0065) or Junie Walker (☎460 0159), one of whom can usually provide you with a vehicle for US$45–75 per day. From December to May, you can rent bicycles for US$20 per day from Jonathan Pereira (☎773 9599, ⊛www.barbudabiketours.net) who has a small fleet of high quality mountain bikes. He also leads hike tours of the island for a reasonable fee of $10 per hour.

Taking a **day tour** is a good way to see the island's sights, including caves and beaches and a boat trip to the bird sanctuary (see p.103). Some reputable local operators are Mr Nedd (☎460 0059), Mr Thomas (☎727 9957) and Devon (☎773 6132) and they each charge about US$60 per person for the day. If you'd like to make a day trip to Barbuda from Antigua, both D&J Tours (☎773 9766) and Jenny's Tours (☎461 9361) will organize a packaged tour for US$170 (via plane) or US$110 (via ferry), including transport to Barbuda, pick-up at the airport or dock, a Jeep tour of the island, lunch and a boat visit to the bird sanctuary. Your driver will also leave you on the beach for as long as you want – just remember to bring plenty of water. Day tours by boat can also be arranged through Tropical Adventures (☎480 1225, ⊛www.tropicalad.com) or the Barbuda Express Ferry (☎764 2291, ⊛www.antiguaferries.com), both of whom travel to Barbuda for snorkelling, birdwatching and beach cruising for around US$120 per person.

though there's little shade here – ask your boatman to drop you near one of the groves of casuarina trees; he'll come back for you a few hours later. Expect to pay about US$20 for a round-trip boat ride from Codrington Pier.

A little further south, **Palmetto Point** features kilometres of sun-speckled beaches and is accessible by road. **White Bay**, down by Cocoa Point, has a beautiful stretch of white sand with good snorkelling. There is public access to this beach right between the *K Club* and *Cow Point* resorts (see p.108).

Just beneath the Indian Caves on the northeast coast (see opposite) along **Two Foot Bay** are several pretty, secluded beaches that are littered with driftwood and other detritus washed up by the Atlantic Ocean. Although they are on the exposed Atlantic side of the island, the beaches are protected by offshore reefs that form

▲ BARBUDAN CAVES

lagoons where you can snorkel and swim.

River Fort

In the southwest of the island, not far from Codrington, you can clamber around some substantial remains at the River Fort, just before *The Beach House* (see p.108). The fort provides a surprisingly large defence for an island of Barbuda's size and importance. The island was attacked by Carib Indians in the 1680s and by the French navy in 1710, but there was too little valuable property here to tempt any further assailants into braving the dangerous surrounding reefs. As a result, the fort never saw any action, and its main role has been as a lookout and a landmark for ships approaching the island from the south.

The fort remains are dominated by a Martello tower, one of the many built throughout the British Empire during the Napoleonic Wars modeled after a tower at Cape Mortella in Corsica – hence the name. Right near the fort, the River Wharf is the main point for access to Barbuda by boat and is always busy with trucks stockpiling and loading sand onto barges to be sold throughout the Caribbean – a very controversial but lucrative industry for the Barbudans.

Spanish Point

Southeast of the River Fort, the road leads out past the upscale but seldom open *K Club* (p.108) to the isolated Spanish Point, where a small finger of land divides the choppy waters of the Atlantic from the calm Caribbean Sea. Maps indicate a castle on Spanish Point, but if you make the effort to get here all you'll find are the ruins of a small lookout post. More interestingly, there is a marine reserve just offshore at Palaster Reef, where numerous shipwrecks have been located in the shallows amid the fabulous coral and abundant reef fish. You can swim to the edges of the reef from the beach, so don't forget your snorkelling gear but beware of currents outside the reef.

Redonda

The little island of Redonda – a two-kilometre hump of volcanic rock rising a sheer 300 metres from the sea – was spotted and named by Columbus in 1493, but subsequently ignored for nearly four centuries. During the 1860s, however, valuable phosphate was found in bird guano there, and Redonda was

Barbuda's shipwrecks

The shallows around Barbuda are littered with historically significant **shipwrecks**, the last resting place for some 150 vessels that failed to navigate safely through the island's dangerous coral reefs. Salvage from the wrecks was an important source of income for the islanders from at least 1695, when the *Santiago de Cullerin* ran aground with 13,000 pesos, destined for paying the garrisons on the Spanish Main in South America. During the following century, ships hitting the reefs included slavers, cargo ships and warships, with the Barbudans recovering everything from cases of brandy to dried codfish, sugar and coal. Income from salvage reached a peak of around £7000 a year by the early 1800s, though improved navigation techniques during the following century saw the number of wrecks decline sharply. To dive these wrecks, contact Dive Barbuda (☎562 3134), a small local dive operation. They can also take you out to dive on some colourful coral reefs on the sheltered southern side of the island.

promptly annexed by Antigua. Mining operations were begun, producing around 4000 tons a year by the end of the century. However, output declined after World War I, the mining ceased and the island has been unoccupied – except by goats and seabirds – since 1930.

Almost surreally, though, Redonda is still claimed as an independent kingdom. In 1865 a Montserratian sea-trader named Matthew Shiell led an expedition to the island and staked his claim to it. His objections to Antigua's annexation of the island were ignored, but it didn't stop him from abdicating in favour of his novelist son in 1880; he in turn passed the fantasy throne to the English poet John Gawsworth, who took the title Juan III and appointed a number of his friends as nobles of the realm, including Dorothy L. Sayers, J.B. Priestley and Lawrence Durrell. Today, a character who styles himself Leo V – actually a history teacher in London – claims to have inherited the kingdom, using his title to promote the literary works of his predecessors. However, at least one pretender to the throne argues that Gawsworth had abdicated in his favour during a night of heavy drinking at his local pub back in England.

Redonda is occasionally visited by sailors and fishermen – though with no sheltered

▼ PALMETTO POINT

▲ TWO FOOT BAY

anchorage, the landing is a difficult one – and there is no regular service to the island, nor anywhere to stay save a few ruined mining buildings when you get there.

Accommodation

The Beach House

Palmetto Point ☎725 4042 or ☎646 495 1668, ⓦwww.thebeachhouse-barbuda.com. Smart hotel on a fantastic beach with twenty rooms, all with a/c and a private patio. The rooms are big, comfortable and stylishly decorated. The Italian chef cooks up top-notch food, much of which (including the bread and pasta) is made fresh on the premises. Prices start at US$750/695 a night in winter/summer including breakfast, dinner and your own personal service ambassador.

The Carriage House

Codrington ☎727 1761, ⒺLNedd@hotmail.co.uk. This pleasant home with tiled floors sits in the centre of town. It offers two bedrooms, each with a private bathroom, a large kitchen and a common area, making it a good option for two couples or a family. The entire house rents for US$75 per night or less for an extended stay.

Coco Point

Coco Point ☎462 3816 local, ☎212 986 1416 in New York, ⓦwww.cocopoint.com. One of the first jet-setter resorts in the Caribbean, with spacious rooms and cottages on a peninsula surrounded by gorgeous beaches with powdery white sand and calm inviting waters. Rates start at US$900/810 per night in winter/summer and include transfer flights between Antigua and Barbuda, three full meals per day, drinks and activities.

Island Chalet

Codrington, behind the Green Door Tavern ☎773 0066 or ☎460 0065. Clean, basic rooms with private hot-water bathrooms and floor fan, for US$88 a night. The four rooms are on the second floor with a small common balcony and a shared kitchen and TV room. *Island Chalet* is right behind one of the more popular bars and might be noisy on weekends.

K Club

Coco Point ☎460 0300, ⓦwww.kclubbarbuda.com. Open Dec–Feb. Stunning Italian-owned and -

designed resort in the south of Barbuda. They're in the process of scaling back their operation and may be closed, so make sure to call ahead. The beautiful white bungalows and villas, all on the beach, start at US$950 per night.

Nedd's Guesthouse

Codrington ☎ 460 0059. This small hotel has a similar design to the *Island Chalet* (opposite), but is a bit more worn down. The upside is that it's just US$50 a night and in a quieter location. To get here, take a right out of the airport and follow the chain-link fence until you reach the two-storey building that's just a few blocks away from the airport.

North Beach

Codrington ☎ 212 689 9688 in New York, ⓦ www.northbeachbarbuda .com. These two simple, comfortable cottages are set on a beautiful remote northern beach of Barbuda and accessible only by boat. Great for a private family getaway. All-inclusive rates start at US$500 per cottage per day.

Restaurants and bars

The Beach House

Palmetto Point ☎ 725 4042, ⓦ www .thebeachhousebarbuda.com. Daily for lunch and dinner. This stylish yet casual spot sits on one of the best beaches in Barbuda and features fresh seafood with a Mediterranean flair and home-made pastas cooked with fresh herbs grown on premises. The four-course dinner is served on the breezy deck and costs US$90 per person. Call ahead to make a reservation if you're staying elsewhere. No shorts after 6pm.

Green Door Tavern

Codrington. Daily 7am–2am. Basic bar with an easy-going vibe and outdoor picnic tables where you can lounge and watch the world go by. Burgers and wings are sometimes served. The owner Byron Askie also rents cars and can help to arrange just about anything you'd like while you're in Barbuda.

▲ VIEW FROM THE BEACH HOUSE

The Lime
Codrington, near the town pier. Friday and Sunday are the big nights here when a DJ, or the occasional live band, gets the locals up and dancing. There may be an EC$10 cover.

Palm Tree
Codrington ☎460 0395. Daily for lunch and dinner. Good island food, particularly for fish and lobster (EC$30–50), but you should let them know in advance that you're coming and what you'd like to eat. Mostly a take-out place in the off season.

Park Terrace Restaurant
Codrington, by the airport ☎460 0092. Mon–Thurs 7am–8pm, Fri & Sat 7am–10pm. Pleasant, clean local diner with breakfast of omelettes and French toast (EC$10–18) and lunch and dinner including sandwiches (EC$10–18) and grilled, curried or stewed meats, seafood and chicken for EC$18–25.

Wa'Omoni's Best
Codrington ☎562 1933. Mon–Sat lunch and dinner. The most sophisticated place in town, with a/c, tinted windows and chilled wine. The friendly staff serves up salads, sandwiches and burgers (including veggie) for EC$8–12 and tasty Barbudan dishes of lobster, conch, pork chops and fresh fish for EC$15–40. The name comes from the original Carib name for Barbuda.

Shops

Art Café
Codrington. On Highland Road heading northeast out of town ☎460 0534. The amiable owners sell local hand-painted silks, prints of island maps, T-shirts and a few other crafts. They also have a wealth of knowledge about the island's natural and cultural sights and they run the ⓦwww.barbudaful.com website.

Authentic Barbudan Souvenirs
Codrington, in the centre of the village ☎460 0614. Proprietor Rose Brooks sells T-shirts and sarongs and also makes traditional dolls and fabric flowers.

Essentials

Arrival

All **flights** to Antigua touch down at V.C. Bird International Airport, on the island's north coast. There is a **limited bus service** from the airport (catch the Coolidge bus to St John's for EC$2.50), but there are numerous car rental outlets at the terminal. **Taxis** – arranged through the dispatch desk – cost around US$16 to Dickenson or Runaway bays, US$11 to St John's or US$31 to English Harbour.

If you arrive by cruise ship, you'll dock at Redcliffe or Heritage quay, in St John's (see p.38 for more on these two quays). From there, you can either take a taxi to anywhere on the island (see "By taxi", p.114); a bus to English Harbour, Parham or Willikies (see "By bus", p.114); or rent a car (see "By car", p.114).

(see p.38 for more on these two quays)

Entry requirements

Citizens of Britain, Ireland, the US, Canada, Australia and New Zealand can enter Antigua without a visa and stay for up to six months. You will, however, need a **passport** (valid for at least six months after the date of onward travel) and a return ticket or proof of onward travel. You might also be asked to show that you have sufficient funds to cover your stay; if you can't satisfy the immigration authorities, they have the right to deny you entry. You will also be asked where you intend to stay, though your answer will not of course be binding.

Island transport

A lot of people come to Antigua, make straight for their hotel and spend the next week or two lying on the beach. For those who want to tour around and see the island, though, there are a variety of options.

Speedy and inexpensive buses run to certain parts of the island, particularly between St John's and English Harbour on the west and south coasts. If you want to explore, you're invariably better off renting a car for a couple of days. If you just want to make the occasional excursion or short trip, hiring taxis can work out to be a better deal.

By bus

The public transport system in Antigua is patchy, with **buses** offering fast, frequent and inexpensive service between St John's and English Harbour, via the centre of the island, and less frequent service to Parham and Willikies on the east coast (from where it's a fifteen-minute walk to the Long Bay beach). There is limited service to the tourist strip of Dickenson Bay on the northwest coast via the #50 bus, and to the airport via the Coolidge bus. Buses and **minibuses** also run along the west coast between St John's and Old Road, stopping off beside several good beaches and the local hotels en route. They also run out to the Five Islands peninsula. For the south and west coasts, buses and minibuses use the West Bus Station near the public market in St John's; for the east coast, they use the east terminal near the Rec (see pp.44 & 39, respectively).

Few of the buses follow any schedule, often departing only when they are full.

Always ask the driver where he's going and tell him well in advance of where you want to get off. Stops are normally marked, though you'll find that the minivans will usually stop anywhere en route. Few buses run after dark or on Sundays.

By car

Antigua is an easy country to **drive** in; driving is on the left, the main roads are mostly good and distances are small. Signposting is abysmal but it's hard to get seriously lost – asking passers-by is the best way to get information if you do. In St John's, though, the streets are narrow and poorly lit, so driving there at night is normally best avoided.

Rental prices start at around US$50 per day, $315 per week; third-party **insurance** is included in the price. If you don't have a credit card that offers free collision damage insurance, you'll have to pay another US$10–20 per day if you want to cover potential damage to the rental car.

When renting a car you'll need to show a current licence from your home country or an international driver's licence. You must also buy a local driving licence for US$20 which is valid for three months and available from the car rental agency. You'll also normally need a credit card to make a security deposit. Consider renting a 4WD if you're staying on the north or east coasts, which have poor roads. Check the car fully to ensure that every dent, scratch or missing part is inventoried and that there is a good spare tyre before you set off. When returning the car, don't forget to collect any credit-card deposit slip.

Reliable firms include Avis (☎ 462 2840), Budget (☎ 462 3009), Dollar (☎ 462 0362), Oakland (☎ 462 3021), Payne (☎ 462 3009) and Thrifty (☎ 462 9532). Each of these can provide you with a car at the airport or deliver one to your hotel.

By taxi

Finding a **taxi** in Antigua – identifiable from a "TX" on their plates – is easy in St John's, Nelson's Dockyard, big resorts or at the airport, but less straightforward in other areas of the island, where you'll often need to call (or ask your hotel to arrange) for one. Fares are regulated according to an official price list that most drivers carry, but there are no meters, so make sure that you agree on a price before you get into the car. At the airport there is a list of government-approved rates: US$11 to St John's, US$16 to Dickenson Bay or Runaway Bay, US$31 to English Harbour. If you rent a taxi for a day's sightseeing, expect to pay around US$20–25 per hour. Two good 24-hour taxi companies are West Bus Station Taxis (☎ 462 5190) and Antigua Reliable (☎ 460 5353).

Cycling and motorbikes

Since Antigua is so small, and there are few steep inclines, it is ideal **cycling** territory, but ride with caution on the roads, particularly when there's traffic. You can rent bikes for as little as US$15 per day, US$80 a week. Hiring a scooter or motorbike is fun but can be dangerous and is discouraged by most hoteliers and expats. Prices start at around US$40 per day or US$225 per week (plus US$20 for the local driving permit). Rental agents can be found on p.125.

Tours

If you fancy leaving the transportation to others, there are a number of local companies that offer island-wide sightseeing **tours**, either to a set itinerary or customized to your desires. Remember to check whether the price includes entrance fees to the various attractions and lunch. Your hotel may also organize tours direct. You can also arrange a private custom tour with some of the taxi operators (see "By taxi," above). For tours to Barbuda, see the box on p.105.

Island Safari (☎ 480 1225, ⓦ www .tropicalad.com) and Estate Safari (☎ 729 1113, ⓦ www.estatesafari.com)

both offer great off-road tours, exploring both the human and natural history of Antigua with lunch and a swimming stop. Island Safari features a good combination package with a jeep tour in the morning, lunch on a deserted beach and a kayaking and snorkelling trip in the afternoon. These tours will each run you about US$85.

Caribbean Helicopters (☎ 460 5900, ⓦ www.caribbeanhelicopters.net) offers sightseeing tours for US$85 per person (15min, half-island tour) or US$150 (30min, full-island tour). Though expensive, it's a great way to see all of Antigua at once – kilometres of shoreline, plus every beach, reef, hotel, and fort, all from an unrivalled bird's-eye view.

Information and maps

Foreign branches of the **Antigua Tourist Office** (ATO) stock plenty of information on the country, including brochures on the main tourist attractions and upcoming events, and a decent road map. Once you're in Antigua, you can get the same information from the Tourist Information booth at Heritage Quay or from the info desk at the airport. For more detailed information, try the friendly Tourism Hospitality Unit (☎ 562 6944/5) at #25 Heritage Quay, upstairs from the vendors' mall. Most of the car rental outlets will also provide you with a free map of the island when you rent from them. A good road map (with topography) is the *International Travel Map: Antigua and Barbuda*, available at The Map Shop in St John's or online (ⓦ www.itmb.com).

You'll find many websites with information on Antigua and Barbuda including the official site of the Department of Tourism, ⓦ www.antigua-barbuda .org, which has good general information, history and travel tips and a very useful calendar of events. Also, ⓦ www.antiguanice.com features up-to-date nightlife listings and a fairly comprehensive directory of businesses catering to tourists. For current information about Barbuda, visit ⓦ www .barbudaful.net.

Antigua has no dedicated listings magazine for music, theatre and other events, though the daily *Antigua Sun* or *Daily Observer* newspapers carry regular arts and events details. Keep an eye also on flyers posted up around the island; local radio stations also announce major events.

Antigua tourist offices overseas

Canada 60 St Clair Ave East, Suite 304, Toronto, Ontario M4T 1N5 ☎ 416/961 3085, ⓕ 416/961-7218.

UK Antigua House, 2nd Floor, 45 Crawford Place, London W1H 4LP ☎ 020/7258 0070 ⓕ 020/7258 3826.

USA 610 5th Ave, Suite 311, New York, NY 10020 ☎ 212/541-4117, ⓕ 212/541-4789, ⓦ www.antigua-barbuda.org

The ATO has no branches in Ireland, Australia or New Zealand.

Money and costs

Antigua is not a particularly cheap country to visit, and prices for many items are at least as much as you'd pay at home. Bargaining is generally frowned upon, but, particularly during the off-season of April to November, it can be worth asking for a reduced rate on items such as accommodation or car rental.

Currency

The island's unit of currency is the **Eastern Caribbean dollar** (EC$), divided into 100 cents. It comes in bills of $100, $50, $20, $10 and $5, as well as coins of $1, $0.50, $0.25, $0.10, $0.05 and $0.01. The rate of exchange is fixed at EC$2.70 to US$1 (at the time of writing, this worked out to roughly EC$5.05 to UK£1 or EC$3.40 to EUR€1), though you'll get a fraction less when you exchange money. In tourist-related business, the US$ is often used as the main currency, and you'll generally find prices for hotels, restaurants and car rental quoted in US$ (a policy we have adopted in this guide). When paying with US dollars or traveller's cheques to pay a bill, you can expect your change to be in EC dollars. Do note that if you use US dollars to buy something advertised in EC dollars, you'll usually get a less than favourable exchange rate, so it's worth carrying some local cash around.

Costs

Accommodation will likely be the major expense of your stay, and most visitors pay this up front as part of a package. Double rooms can start as low as US$45/£24 a night for a simple room away from the beach. On the beach, the cheapest options clock in at US$100–150/£53–80 in high season (winter), or US$85–125/£45–67 in low season (summer). All-inclusives start in the neighbourhood of US$200/£110 or so a night (many with a minimum-stay requirement), and only go up from there:

some exclusive resorts cost well over $1200/£640 a night. Keep in mind, too, that every place adds government tax of 8.5 percent onto the total bill, and that almost all add a service charge of 10 percent.

Aside from room costs, a realistic daily budget, including a decent meal out, the occasional taxi ride and a bit of evening entertainment, begins at about US$75/£40 – but really the sky's the limit.

Traveller's cheques and ATM and credit cards

The safest method of carrying money is in the form of **traveller's cheques**. While sterling and other currencies are perfectly valid and accepted in the island's banks, US dollar traveller's cheques – due to the fixed rate between US and EC dollars – are the best ones to have. They are available for a small commission from most banks, and from branches of American Express and Thomas Cook; make sure you keep the purchase agreement and a record of cheque serial numbers safe and separate from the cheques themselves. Once in Antigua, the cheques can be cashed at banks (you'll need your passport or other photo ID to validate them) for a small charge.

ATM cards are also a safe and convenient means to obtain money while travelling. Your card should be accepted at most bank machines in Antigua (though to be sure, confirm with your home bank that your PIN number will work abroad). You'll get cash at the bank's official rate of exchange which is about as good as it gets. The highest concentration of ATMs is in St John's. Further away, they can be hard to find; there is only one ATM in the English/Falmouth Harbour area, for example.

Major credit cards – American Express, Visa, MasterCard – are widely accepted, but don't necessarily expect the smaller hotels and restaurants to take them. You can also use the cards to get cash advances at most banks, though you'll pay both commission to the bank and hefty interest to your credit card company. Also note that vendors will often add on three to five percent of the price of something if paid on a credit card.

Banking hours

Banking hours are generally Mon–Thurs 8am–3pm, Fri 8am–5pm; branches of the Bank of Antigua are also open on Saturday from 8am to noon (see p.129 for locations). Many **hotels** will also exchange money, though if you're changing anything other than US$ the rate is usually a bit worse than the banks.

Wiring money

If you run out of money, and have lost your ATM and credit cards, you can have someone at home **wire you money**, via either Western Union (Ⓦ www.westernunion.com) or MoneyGram (Ⓦ www.emoneygram .com). Expect a charge of about US$15 to send US$100. You can pick up the money from any Western Union or MoneyGram agent on the island. Both companies have agents in St John's, Western Union on Long Street near Thames (Mon–Sat 8.30am–5pm; ☎562 6445) and MoneyGram at *Joe Mike's Hotel* on Corn Alley by Nevis Street (Mon–Fri 9am–4.30pm, Sat 9am–3pm; ☎462 0491).

Communications and the media

Antigua's **postal service** is reasonably efficient. The GPO in St John's is open Mon–Fri 8am–4pm (5pm Fri) and has poste restante (general delivery) facilities for receiving mail. There are also branches at the airport, at the Woods Centre and at English Harbour, and you can buy stamps and send mail at many of the hotels. **Postal rates** are reasonable: to the USA and Canada, air mail is EC$1.50, postcards EC$0.75; to the UK and Australasia, air mail is EC$1.80, postcards EC$0.90.

Calling within Antigua is simple – most hotels provide a **telephone** in each room (though be wary of surcharges). You'll also see **phone booths** all over the island, and these can be

International calls

To phone Antigua from abroad, dial your international access code (UK ☎001, Ireland ☎001, Australia ☎0011, New Zealand ☎00; from the US or Canada, just dial ☎1) then 268 + seven-digit number.

To phone abroad from Antigua, dial the international access code (☎011 when calling the UK, Ireland, Australia, or New Zealand; unnecessary when calling the US or Canada), your country code (UK ☎44, Ireland ☎353, USA ☎1, Canada ☎1, Australia ☎61, New Zealand ☎64) + area code (minus first 0, if there is one) + number.

used for local and international calls. Most of the booths take phonecards only – which are available at hotels, post offices and some shops. If you want to use your **mobile phone**, you can usually roam using the national APUA network. Charges are likely to be high so be sure to check with your service provider before leaving home. Otherwise you can rent a phone from APUA (☎ 727 2782). For looking up phone numbers, hotel rooms and phone booths often have a **directory**; failing that, call directory assistance on ☎ 411. To reach the operator dial ☎ 0.

Newspapers and radio

As always, local newspapers and radio are a great way to find out what's on the nation's mind. Check out the *Daily Observer, or the Antigua Sun*, the main paper concentrating on domestic news but with a decent section on news from the wider Caribbean and the rest of the world and, invariably, a big sports section. There are several radio stations on both AM and FM that carry religious shows, news, sport, call-in shows and music, mostly international hits with a sprinkling of local tunes.

Accommodation

Many visitors book their accommodation as part of a package deal, to get the best rates possible; you can get hooked up with a casual guesthouse, an apartment or a plusher resort, depending on your wants.

A significant and growing number of accommodation options are **all-inclusive** hotels. The simple concept behind these places is that you pay a single price that covers your room, all meals and, normally, all drinks and watersports. If you're thinking of booking an all-inclusive, focus on what you specifically want out of it. *Sandals* and the giant *Jolly Beach Resort*, for example, have several restaurants and bars, so you don't have to face the same menu every night, while smaller places like *Rex Blue Heron* offer less variety, but a bit more space on the beach (for reviews of these three places, see pp.56 & 97, respectively). Remember, too, that the allure of drinking seven types of "free" cocktail in a night or stuffing your face at the "free" buffet quickly fades, especially if you want to get out and sample Antigua's great restaurants and bars.

A good option for many are the smaller locally owned hotels such as the *Siboney Beach Club* or The *Catamaran Hotel* and the top-quality restaurants like *Chez Pascal* and *Harmony Hall* that also offer accommodation (for reviews of these four places, see pp. 56, 83, 98 & 69, respectively). Some of the independent hotels on the island have also banded together in a venture called VIP, or Very Intimate Places (ⓦ www.antigua-vip.com), which offers a range of suitable accommodation. Another possibility is the Vacation Rentals by Owner website (ⓦ www.vrbo.com) which lists a variety of mostly private homes for rent, from simple studios to luxurious waterfront estates.

Wherever we've listed accommodations, we've quoted **prices** for the least expensive double room during high season (mid-December to mid-April, aka winter) alongside, where applicable, prices for the least expensive double during low season (mid-April to mid-December, aka summer). Some of the upscale hotels charge an even higher rate over Christmas and New Years or during Sailing Week (see p.77).

The island's standard **electrical current** is 110 volts with two-pin sockets, though a few of the older hotels still use 220 volts.

Food and drink

There are plenty of good eating options on Antigua and, though prices can be on the high side, there's usually something to suit most budgets. Around most of the island, hotel and restaurant menus aimed at tourists tend to offer familiar variations on Euro-American-style food, shunning local specialities – a real shame, as the latter are usually excellent and well worth trying if you get the chance. Away from the posh hotels, restaurants and bars can be low-key and, like the overall pace of life, slow. If you're heading to Barbuda, don't expect the same level of choice and sophistication as on Antigua.

Traditional Antiguan food

Almost everywhere, breakfast is based around coffee, cereal, toast and eggs, and will usually include fresh fruit, one of the country's strong points. Expect to find paw-paws (papayas), bananas and the sweet (and often tiny) Antiguan black pineapple year-round. While in season – generally between May and August – make a special effort to look out for the delicious local mangoes and sapodillas.

For other meals you'll find that seafood – as you'd expect – is one of the island's strong points. Of the fish, the tasty and versatile red snapper and grouper are the staples but, if you're lucky, you'll come across swordfish, mahi mahi (also called dolphin) and the very meaty marlin on the menu. Lobster is usually the priciest item, anywhere from EC$45–100 depending on season and the type of establishment. You'll also find conch (pronounced "konk") – a large shellfish often curried, stewed or battered in fritters, though best of all eaten raw in conch salad, when it's finely chopped with hot and sweet peppers, cucumber and lemon juice – as well as the giant local cockles and whelks, usually served in a buttery garlic sauce.

Other Antiguan specialities include the fabulous ducana (a solid hunk of grated sweet potato mixed with coconut and spices and steamed in a banana leaf); pepperpot stew (salt beef, pumpkin and okra) often served with a cornmeal pudding known as fungi; goat or conch water (tender stewed goat or conch cooked with onions, butter, chives, thyme, cloves and browning, served with bread to mop up the gravy); various types of curry; salted codfish; and souse – cuts of pork marinated in lime juice, onions, hot and sweet peppers and spices. Roti, a sandwich of curried potatoes and meat or vegetables wrapped in flaky thin bread, while originally from Trinidad, is found throughout the island at local eateries and is cheap and delicious.

Vegetarians will find their choices limited – there are some great vegetables grown on Antigua, including pumpkins, okra and the squash-like christophene, but many menus don't include a single vegetarian dish, and even the widely available rice and peas often contains a piece of salted pork. Your best bet is probably to phone ahead and see if there are any truly vegetarian options; otherwise, opt for self-catering.

Drinking

For **drinking**, Wadadli is the local beer, a reasonable brew though not quite a match for the superb Red Stripe, a Jamaican beer brewed under licence on the island. Other regular beers on offer include Heineken, Guinness and the Trinidadian Carib. Rum is the most popular spirit, used as the basis for a range of cocktails from piña coladas to rum punch (unique to each bar). The English Harbour and Cavalier brands are both made on the island and are quite good, though real aficionados of the stuff will want to look out for Mount Gay Extra Old from Barbados, Haitian Barbancourt or Brugal (Extra Viejo) from the Dominican Republic, all very good Caribbean rums, best served neat on ice.

As for **soft drinks**, you'll find the usual brands of sodas as well as the tasty sparkling real grapefruit drink Ting, made locally, and a range of delicious local drinks made from passion fruit, tamarind, lime, guava or soursop. If you're visiting mid-winter try to find the bright red sorrel drink, made from seasonal hibiscus flowers. Look out, too, for vendors standing by piles of green coconuts; for a couple of EC dollars they'll cut the top off one for you to drink the sweet, delicious water inside. Tap water, and thus ice cubes, in Antigua are perfectly safe to consume. You can also opt for bottled water which is available everywhere. Barbudan water, while also safe, is fairly brackish and so it's best to drink bottled water when you're there.

Restaurant costs and hours

If a service charge is not added to your bill, you should tip ten to fifteen percent.

Opening hours are fairly standard – lunch typically from noon until 2 or 2.30pm, and dinner from 6pm. Bear in mind that many of the smaller restaurants close the kitchen early (around 9pm), particularly when business is slow. Additionally, some restaurants close for a couple of months over the summer, sometimes on a whim, depending on how quiet the season is expected to be.

During the winter season (Dec–April) it's worth making a reservation at many of the more upscale restaurants; if you've got your heart set on a special place, you should probably arrange it a couple of days in advance. And finally, a word on **prices**: some restaurants quote their prices in EC$, others in US$, others in both. We've followed their practice, using whichever currency a particular restaurant quotes.

Ocean and beach safety

No shots are needed before heading to Antigua – the major tropical diseases were eradicated long ago – and you'll find that the only real threat to your physical welfare is the intense **Caribbean sun**. Many visitors get badly sunburned on the first day and suffer for the rest of the trip. To avoid this fate, it's advisable to wear a strong sunscreen at all times; if you're after a tan, start strong and gradually reduce the factor. As for exposure times, fifteen minutes a day in the early morning or late afternoon is recommended, if rarely followed; sunworshippers should at least avoid the heat of the day between 11am and 2pm. If you do get sunburned, try the **aloe vera** gel that's available at the island's pharmacies (see "Directory", p.129, for a list of these). The aloe plant itself is found

all over the island and is recognizable as a knee-high plant consisting of thick, swollen light-green spikes pointing upward; just tear off one of these limbs and rub the gooey juice on your burn.

While you're on the beach, steer clear of the **Manchineel trees**, recognizable by their shiny dark green leaves and small, crab apple-like fruits. The fruit is poisonous and the bark and leaves give off a poisonous sap that will cause blisters if it gets on you. The sea, too, poses a handful of threats. Don't worry about the rarely seen sharks or barracudas, which won't spoil your visit, but watch out for spiny black **sea urchins**. They're easily missed if you're walking over a patch of sea grass or among rocks; if you step on one and can't get the spines completely out, you'll need medical help.

You should also avoid touching any jellyfish or coral; the contact does the animals no good and may cause you stings or infections. Finally, mosquitoes and tiny sandflies can be an occasional problem, particularly on the beach in early evening; take **insect repellent** to keep them at bay.

Sport and outdoor activities

The beach addict and the watersports fanatic are equally at home in Antigua, with a variety of great beaches to choose from and plenty of operators offering excellent diving, snorkelling, waterskiing and other activities. Also on the water, a number of companies offer trips along the coast by boat or catamaran, and you can charter boats for deep-sea fishing. There are plenty of land-based options, too, with a couple of good golf courses, a horse-riding stable and hiking, mountain-biking and jeep trips.

Although diving options around Antigua are best in the south, the northwest coast is probably the best spot for general watersports; **Dickenson Bay** in particular has several reputable operators at its northern end. The sea is pretty calm here year-round and, beyond the protected swimming zone, you can waterski, windsurf, parasail or jet-ski. **Paradise Reef**, a half-kilometre-long coral garden to the north of the bay, is a popular spot for glass-bottom boat trips and snorkelling, and there are good coralheads offshore around tiny **Prickly Pear Island**, a short boatride to the northeast.

Barbuda surpasses even Antigua in the quality (and remoteness) of its beaches, and its snorkelling and diving opportunities are also world-class. Unfortunately, the island has little in the way of infrastructure to support tourists looking for watersports – but scuba diving and fishing options do exist.

Diving and snorkelling

Diving is excellent on the coral reefs around Antigua and Barbuda, with most of the good sites – places like Sunken Rock and Cape Shirley – on the south side of the larger island. Many of these sites are very close to shore, rarely more than a fifteen-minute boat ride away. Expect to see a wealth of fabulously colourful reef fish, including parrot fish, angelfish, wrasse and barracuda, as well as the occasional harmless nurse shark and, if you're lucky, dolphins and turtles. The reefs for the most part are still in very good condition and, though there is no wall diving and most dives are fairly shallow, there are some good cliffs and canyons and a handful of wrecks.

Antigua has plenty of quality dive operators scattered conveniently around the island, so you should always be able to find a boat going out from near where you're staying. Rates are pretty uniform: reckon on around US$100 for a two-tank dive with equipment. Beginners can get a feel for diving by taking a half-day resort course, which covers basic theory and includes a shallow-water (or pool) demonstration and a single reef dive. The course costs around US$100, and allows you to continue to dive with the people who taught you, though not with any other operator (as you're not really certified). Full open-water certification – involving theory, tests, training dives and four full dives – is rather more variable in price, costing US$400–500, depending on the time of year and how busy the operator is.

Serious divers should consider a **package deal**, either involving a simple three or five two-tank dive package (ie, three or five separate trips, consisting of two dives each; roughly US$200–300 and US$350–450, respectively) or a deal that includes accommodation and diving. Prices for these can be pretty good value, particularly outside the winter season. It's worth contacting the dive operators directly to find out the latest offers.

Barbuda's diving is at least as good as Antigua's, with countless wrecks dotted around the nearby reefs (see p.107 for more on Barbuda's shipwrecks). Dive Barbuda (☎ 562 3134), a small new dive outfit, can take you diving on some of these wrecks and also on the beautiful coral reefs on the more protected western side of the island.

Snorkelling around the islands is excellent, too, and several of the dive operators take snorkellers on their dive trips, mooring near some good, relatively shallow coral heads. Plan on around US$20–25 for an outing, including equipment. That said, a boat ride is far from essential for snorkellers – there are loads of good spots just a short swim offshore from both Antigua and Barbuda, and these are mentioned throughout the Guide. Most of the top hotels have snorkelling gear for hire or loan, but if you're not at one of these, finding the equipment can be tricky. Check with your nearest dive shop, or you can purchase gear at Aquasports at Heritage Quay in Antigua (☎ 480 3090). It's worth bringing a mask and fins with you, certainly if you're heading to Barbuda.

Dive operators

Antigua Scuba Centre Long Bay ☎ 729 4698, ☜ www.antiguascuba.com. Dive shop offering small boats (meaning fewer other divers), close dive sites and PADI certification courses. US$80 for two dives with equipment.

Aquanauts English Harbour ☎ 460 2813. Good, professional south coast outfit with decent equipment, catering to drop-ins from around the island.

Dive Antigua At the *Rex Halcyon Cove* hotel, Dickenson Bay ☎ 462 3483, ☜ www .diveantigua.com. Based on the northwest coast, Dive Antigua is the longest-established and best-known dive operation on the island; prices are normally a little higher than most of the other operators. They also offer a glass-bottomed boat to take snorkellers out to the reef.

Dockyard Divers Nelson's Dockyard ☎ 460 1178 or 729 3040. Decent-sized dive shop that offers diving trips around the south and west coasts.

Jolly Dive Jolly Harbour Marina ☎ 462 8305, ☜ www.jollydive.com. Second-oldest dive shop in Antigua, recommended by locals and very popular with guests at nearby hotels. Offering numerous levels of training. A two-tank dive with equipment costs US$100.

Ultramarine At the *Sunsail Club Colonna* resort, Hodges Bay and at the *St James Club*, Mamora Bay ☎ 562 5062. Good dive shop, with locations on the north and southwest coasts of the island. As well as regular dive trips, they also offer "surface scuba" for children aged 5–12. They're a bit pricey at US$115 for two dives with equipment, but they've also earned a PADI Five Star Gold Palm designation for safety and quality.

Boats and catamarans

There is no shortage of boat and catamaran trips to be made around Antigua, with the emphasis on being part of a big crowd all having a fun time together – not, it must be said, everyone's cup of tea. Most of the cruises charge a single price, including a meal and all the drinks you want, and the two main cruise companies, Kokomo and Wadadli Cats, offer virtually identical trips, travelling on large, comfortable catamarans.

The most popular cruise – a great way to see the island – sails right around Antigua, taking in some snorkelling and lunch at Green Island off the east coast.

There is also a superb snorkelling trip to Cades Reef on the south coast, stopping off for lunch on one of the west coast beaches, and another to uninhabited Great Bird Island – where there's plenty of bird life – off the northeast. Finally, there's a "triple destination" cruise on Sundays to English Harbour via Green Island, ending with a taxi ride up to the steel band party on Shirley Heights and another taxi home.

Each of these trips is offered by Kokomo and Wadadli, and both will pick up passengers from a number of different locations on the west coast. All are out from around 9am until 4pm, apart from the triple-destination tour, which runs roughly 9am to sunset. The circumnavigation cruise costs US$95 per person, Cades Reef US$80, and the triple-destination cruise US$110, all prices including snorkelling gear, a buffet lunch and an open bar. Tickets for children under 12 are half-price and infants are free.

Cruise and boat tour operators

Adventure Antigua ☎726 6355, ⓕ560 4672, ⓦwww.adventureantigua .com. Owner Eli Fuller takes passengers by motorboat on a seven-hour ecotour of the northeast coast of the island, showing where the endangered hawksbill turtles lay their eggs, and through the mangrove swamps, looking out for rays, frigate birds, osprey and turtles. There are several snorkelling opportunities, and the guide lays on fresh fruit juices, rum punch and lunch on a deserted beach. Cost is US$100 per person, and the trip goes out between two and five times a week, depending on demand. In stark contrast, they also offer the Xtreme Circumnavigation, which races around the island in a *Miami Vice*-style boat with lots of bumpy high-speed thrills, five stops, lunch and drinks for US$170 – this is clearly not for everyone.

Excellence and Tiami ☎480 1225, ⓦwww.tropicalad.com. On sleek, luxurious new catamarans, trips around the island or to Cades Reef, Great Bird Island or Barbuda. Costs from US$85 per person.

Jabberwocky ☎775 0595 or 773 3115, ⓦwww.adventurecaribbean.com. Tailor-made day, overnight or multi-day cruises on a luxurious charter yacht. Pick whichever beaches and coves you want to visit around the island or even go overnight to Barbuda. Costs from US$85 per person including food and drinks. A three-night trip to Guadeloupe for six people costs US$3000. Book early.

Kokomo Cats ☎462 7245, ⓦwww .kokomocat.com. Round the island trips (Tues, Thurs, & Sat, US$85), Cades Reef (Wed, US$70), Great Bird Island (Fri, US$70), and a quadruple-destination cruise (no different from a triple-destination cruise; Sun, $100) on speedy, well-appointed catamarans. Kokomo also offer sunset cruises on Thursdays from Jolly Harbour on the west coast, departing at 4.30pm (US$40).

"Paddles" Kayak & Snorkel Club ☎463 1944, ⓦwww.antiguapaddles.com. Based in the village of Seatons on the northeast coast, this outfit offers half-day ecotours of mangroves, reefs and the local coast via motor boat, kayak, snorkelling and a nature walk for US$50 per person.

Sunsail Antigua Charters Nelson's Dockyard ☎460 2615. Day-long sailing charters on a variety of yachts with a skipper who will bring you where you want and teach you how to sail. A boat for 6 people costs US$600 per day and a catamaran that holds up to 10 people costs US$700.

Wadadli Cats ☎462 4792, ⓦwww .wadadlicats.com. Circumnavigation cruises (Tues, Thurs, Sat, US$95), Cades Reef (Wed, US$80), Great Bird Island (Fri, US$80), and a triple-destination cruise on Sunday (US$110).

Sailing

Antigua is one of the prime sailing destinations in the Caribbean and, particularly during Sailing Week in April/May, the island becomes a refuelling and party stop for crowds of hearty yachters. If you're after some crewing on boats sailing between the West Indian islands, ask around and look out for crew notices at Jolly Harbour, Falmouth Harbour and Nelson's Dockyard. The charter yacht companies (see p.124) sometimes have crew listings as well. For information on Sailing Week and the preceding classic yacht regatta, see the box on p.77 and check out ⓦwww.sailingweek.com and ⓦwww.antiguaclassics.com.

Yachting charters

Chartering a **yacht** has become a very popular way to explore Caribbean islands. You can choose from among several sizes and styles of motor or sailing vessels and, depending on your needs and experience, you can hire just the boat (bareboat) or you can add in a captain or a full crew including a chef. Fully crewed, all-inclusive rates are comparable to the prices at all-inclusive resorts.

If you fancy yourself a sailor, and have the experience and skills to back it up, you can rent a 36- to 50-foot sailboat (without any crew) through Horizon Yacht Charters (☎ 562 4725 🔽 www .horizonyachtcharters.com). A 40-foot sailboat that sleeps six people starts at US $1995 per week, which works out to about US$50 per person per day. You can hire a skipper through them if you need help.

For a fully crewed charter experience, contact Nicholson's Yacht Charters (☎ 460 1530, 🔽 www.nicholson-charters .com). An all-inclusive week-long charter for four people aboard a 48-foot sailing yacht, starts at around US$7000. You will have the option of visiting the neighbouring islands of St. Kitts, Nevis, Guadeloupe and St. Martin. In the Wild Adventures (🔽 www.inthewild.org) also offers unique crewed sailing experiences throughout the Eastern Caribbean including Antigua.

Fishing

Various charter boats offer deep-sea fishing trips where you can go after wahoo, tuna, barracuda, snook, tarpon, bone fish and, if you're lucky, marlin and sailfish. Prices for up to six people start at around US$500 for a half-day, $800 for a whole day, including rods, bait, food, drink and transport from your hotel. If you want to go on your own, operators will put you with another group if they can and charge around US$100 for a half-day.

Regular operators include Missa Ferdie (☎ 462 1440, 🖂 shoulj@candw.ag), Night-wing (☎ 464 4665, 🔽 www.fishantigua .com, 🖂 nwing31@hotmail.com),

Overdraft (☎ 463 3112 or 464 4954, 🔽 www.antiguafishing.com, 🖂 nunesb@ candw.ag) and Adventure Fishing Charters (☎ 723 6070, 🖂 sushihunter@hotmail .com). If you hunt around at dockside, particularly in St John's and Jolly Harbour, you can find plenty of others.

If you just want to go out with some local fishermen – which can be an amazing experience – ask around at one of the main fishing settlements like Old Road on the south coast. Many will be grateful for an extra pair of hands, though you'll need to clarify in advance exactly what's expected of you – pulling lobster pots and fishing nets is extremely tough work and you may be at it for hours.

Other watersports

Many of the hotels have their own **windsurfers** which you can borrow for no extra cost, and there's a windsurfing school (daily 9am–5pm) at *Sunsail Club Colonna* (see p.68) on the northeast coast. Non-guests can buy a day's watersports pass for US$50, or US$25 for a half (both allow you to attend the windsurfing school).

A little further east and not far from the airport, Dutchman's Bay is another good spot for windsurfing, whether you're a beginner or an expert. H2O Antigua (☎ 562 3933 or 773 9463) rents equipment for US$60 a day, with lessons starting at US$50.

On Dickenson Bay, Tony's Water Sports (☎ 462 6326), Sea Sports (☎ 462 3355) and Pop's (☎ 460 5644) offer a variety of watersports. A ten-minute **parasail** costs US$45, a similar period of **waterskiing** costs US$25, while **jet-skis** cost US$30 for half an hour (US$40 for a two-seater). If you want to do a lot of watersports, consider buying a day-pass for around US$35 from *Rex Halcyon Cove* or US$100 from *Sandals* (see p.56). You'll also find various people offering use of their jet-skis and small sailboats at negotiable prices; it usually works out cheaper than going with an established company

– but bear in mind that insurance will be non-existent.

Lastly, at Jabberwock Beach on the north coast, you can try the new sport of **kiteboarding** with an outfit called KiteAntigua (☎727 3983 or 460 3414, ⓦwww.kiteantigua.com) – see p.62 for more information.

Golf

There are two eighteen-hole public golf courses in Antigua.

Golf courses

Cedar Valley Golf Club 5km north of St John's ☎462 0161, ⓕ562 2762, ⓦwww.cedarvalleygolf.ag, ⓔcedarvalley @candw.ag. A 6157-yard, par 70 championship course, and venue for the annual Antigua Open, held each November. It's a lovely course, lined with palms, flamboyants and cedars and, from its higher points, offers great panoramic views of the island. Given the dryness of the islands, water hazards are mercifully few but, that aside, it's a reasonably challenging course. Greens fees are US$35 for eighteen holes (US$18 for nine holes), plus US$20 per person for rental of clubs and another US$30 if you want to rent a cart (US$15 for nine holes). The dress code is pretty relaxed, but you will need a collared shirt.

Jolly Harbour Golf Course 8km south of St John's ☎462 3085, ⓦwww.jollyharbourantigua.com/golf.html. The island's other major golf location, a 6001-yard, par 71 course designed by American Karl Litten. It's an excellent course, flatter than Cedar Valley but (with seven lakes) more fraught with peril. Plan on US$50 for eighteen holes or US$30 for nine, US$25/15 for club rentals for 18/9 holes, and US$35/20 for a cart for 18/9 holes.

Horseback riding

Though you may well be offered a horseback tour during your visit especially on the southern end of Dickenson Bay, there is only one official horse-riding stable on the island, located just west of Falmouth at Spring Hill (☎460 7787 or 773 3139, ⓦwww.springhillridingclub.com). They have around a dozen horses

and offer lessons and riding tours of the area for about US$40.

Tennis and squash

Many hotels on Antigua have their own tennis courts, best at places like the *Royal Antiguan*, *Rex Halcyon Cove* and the *St James Club*, but there are a handful of public tennis and squash courts available around the island, charging EC$45 per hour, and EC$5 for hire of equipment.

Tennis and squash courts

BBR Sportive Jolly Harbour ☎462 6260. Private squash and four floodlit tennis courts at this west coast resort; rackets and other equipment can be hired.

Temo Sports English Harbour ☎463 6376. Two glass-backed squash courts and two floodlit synthetic-grass tennis courts, with all equipment available for hire. There's also a burger bar and a good bar area with pool and darts. Round-robin tennis tournament on Fridays; closed Saturday evenings and Sundays.

Cycling

Cycling is a great way of seeing Antigua, not least because there are few hills and – away from St John's – not much traffic either. Operators offer guided island tours by mountain bike, particularly through attractive places like Fig Tree Drive in the south; if you want to go it alone, several outfits will be happy to rent you a bike sans guide.

Cycle companies

Bikes Plus Independence Ave, St John's ☎462 2453 or 462 6050. They rent a variety of bikes for US$15 per day or US$90 per week. Inquire here about bike tours of Antigua.

H2O Antigua Dutchman's Bay, Coolidge ☎562 3933 or ☎773 9463. Mountain bikes can be rented from this windsurfing centre for US$35 for a day, US$105 for a week.

Paradise Boat Sales Jolly Harbour ☎460 7125. Bikes rented for US$15 per day, US$70 for a week.

Cricket in Antigua

If you're in Antigua for any length of time, you'll find it almost impossible to avoid the subject of **cricket** – the true national passion. If you're lucky, there'll be a game at the Rec during your stay; if so, don't miss the chance to check out the calypso atmosphere. Failing that, expect at least to get roped into a game of beach cricket, where you'll find fielders standing under the palm trees and in the sea waiting for a miscued shot.

Cricket arrived in Antigua via the British military in the mid-nineteenth century. The 59th Foot Regiment formed the island's first club on New Year's Day 1842, and the *Antigua Times* recorded an Antigua XI beaten by the crew of the *HMS Phaeton* at Shirley Heights on September 26, 1863. For decades, cricket clubs remained the preserve of the ruling class: strictly whites-only and often little more than extended social clubs for the planters and merchants. But, despite the early snobbery that was attached to the game, it soon began to catch on in the sugar estates, where the workers drew up their own pitches and organized matches.

In 1895 Antigua received its first overseas touring team, who reported playing against a home team composed entirely of "coloured" players. (On the same tour, by comparison, the authorities in Barbados excluded black players from their team, irrespective of merit). In 1920 the Rising Sun Cricket Club was founded for poor men in St John's, and by the 1930s – half a century before independence – Antigua had its first black sporting hero in the batsman **Pat Nanton**.

Nonetheless, Antigua remained a cricketing minnow well into the twentieth century, with the regional game dominated by the "Big Four" cricket nations: Jamaica, Barbados, Trinidad and Guyana. In 1966 the Caribbean Shell Shield competition was established for those four and a fifth team – the Combined Islands – made up of players from Antigua and the other small islands. Rarely taken seriously during the 1970s, this Combined Islands team swept to victory in the Shield in 1981, the year of Antigua's independence, led by the brilliant Antiguan **Viv Richards** (see box, p.42). From that time, the Combined Islands team was allowed to become two – the Leeward Islands of the northeastern Caribbean (dominated by Antigua) and the Windward Islands of the southeast (including Grenada, St Vincent and St Lucia) – with the Leewards team consistently performing well in both the Shield and the one-day Red Stripe Cup, inaugurated in 1982.

Somewhat surprisingly, given the importance of cricket on Antigua, no Antigua-specific cricket website exists. For now, the best way to find out information on matches is via the generalized websites (ⓦ www.cricinfo.com or ⓦ www.windiescricket.com).

Hiking

There are plenty of great hikes in Antigua, especially to the hilltop forts, a number of which are described throughout the Guide. For hiking in the English Harbour area, pick up the *Guide to the Hiking Trails in the National Parks* at the entrance to Nelson's Dockyard, or find the same information on the museum's website (ⓦ www.antiguamuseums.org). The local Environmental Awareness Group (☎ 462 6236) leads hikes and bird-watching trips on the third weekend of most months; call them to see what's planned. Peter Todd who formerly ran The Hiking Company (☎ 720 3666) might be convinced to do an occasional longer hike.

Crime and personal safety

Compared to what you'll encounter in Jamaica or several other Caribbean islands, harassment in Antigua is extremely mild. The itinerant vendors who patrol some of the beaches are the main culprits – you'll occasionally be offered drugs or pressed to look at some uninspiring crafts – but on the whole police crackdowns have kept them at a distance. If you're not interested, just be firm in saying no thanks and they'll leave you alone. Petty theft on beaches and from rental cars is not uncommon, so take care with your belongings.

Violent **crime** involving tourists is rare but not unheard of. After dark, it's advisable to steer clear of unlit or unpatrolled areas of the beach, and you'll probably want to avoid the rougher areas of St John's, though there's no reason why you'd want to visit them. **Drugs** present an increasing problem on the island, particularly a growing use of crack cocaine, which is leading to a rise in theft and burglary to finance the habit. Marijuana use is even more widespread – and also illegal – often distributed on the beaches, particularly on the south coast, to likely-looking candidates. If you want it, you can get it, but bear in mind that there are plenty of undercover police around, and the local press runs stories daily of tourists facing heavy fines for possession.

Travelling with children

Calm, clear seas, shelving beaches, no serious health risks and a welcoming attitude make Antigua an ideal destination for babies, toddlers and children. Most hotels welcome families and give substantial discounts for children – those under 12 often stay free in their parents' room – but it's worth checking in advance whether they put any restrictions on kids, especially if you're heading for an all-inclusive; *Sandals*, for example, only accepts couples.

You may also want to check into babysitting/childminding facilities. Child-friendly places like *Sunsail Club Colonna* (see p.68) have wonderful daytime activities and clubs where you can drop off kids of all ages. Many others have games rooms and sports equipment like sailboats and kayaks that will keep older children entertained for hours in a safe environment.

Festivals and events

The main events in Antigua are the summertime **Carnival** and April's **Sailing Week**, but there are various other events to distract you from the beach, including international **cricket**, **tennis** and **warri** (a board game) tournaments. The local and overseas tourist boards (see p.115) have full details of all the activities.

Barbuda's version of carnival, **Caribana**, is held during the Pentecost weekend (seven Sundays after Easter). It's a great time to visit as the island livens up with music shows, calypso competitions, a beauty pageant, a seafood festival and a beach barbeque with live bands. Note that Barbuda gets flooded with Antiguans during this weekend, and accommodations become scarce, so plan accordingly.

Annual events

January

Official start of West Indian cricket season Antigua Cricket Association ☎ 462 9090, Ⓦ www.windiescricket.com. See box p.126.

February

Valentine's Day Regatta Jolly Harbour ☎ 461 6324. A two-day event consisting of four yacht classes and seven short races.

March–April

Test cricket ☎ 462 9090, Ⓦ www .cricinfo.com and Ⓦ www.windiescricket .com. International cricket matches take place at the Rec grounds and in the future perhaps at the new Sir Vivian Richards Stadium.

April–May

Classic Yacht Regatta ☎ 460 1799, Ⓦ www.antiguaclassics.com. A series of parties and sailing races that celebrate the spirit of and appreciation for classic yachts. Held just before Sailing Week.

Sailing Week ☎ 462 8872, Ⓦ www .sailingweek.com. See box p.77.

May

Tennis Week At the *Curtain Bluff Hotel* ☎ 462 8400. International tennis gathering with instructional sessions and world-class matches.

May–June

Sport Fishing Tournament At the *Catamaran Marina*, Falmouth Harbour ☎ 460 7400, Ⓦ www.antiguabarbudasportfishing .com. Local and visiting sport fishermen compete for cash prizes and trophies with their largest fish.

Caribana Codrington, Barbuda ☎ 460 0077. Barbuda's version of carnival.

July–August

Carnival ☎ 462 4707, Ⓦ www .antiguacarnival.com. See box p.40.

October

National Warri Festival ☎ 480 5770. National competition for this ancient game that aficionados rank alongside chess, bridge and backgammon.

Public holidays

New Year's Day	Jan 1
Good Friday	Fri before Easter Sunday
Easter Monday	day after Easter Sunday
Labour Day	first Mon in May
Whit Monday	end of May (varies)
Caricom Day	July 5
Carnival	first Mon and Tues in Aug
United Nations Day	first Mon in Oct
Independence Day	Nov 1
Christmas Day	Dec 25
Boxing Day	Dec 26

December

Nicholson's Annual Charter Yacht Show ☎ 460 1530, ⓦ www .antigua-charter-yacht-meeting.com. The world's oldest charter yacht show sees boats from all over the world converge on English Harbour and Falmouth – from sloops and cutters to schooners and catamarans, plus big power craft.

Directory

Unless otherwise stated, all services listed are in St John's.

Airlines American Airlines ☎ 462 0950; British Airways ☎ 462 0876; BWIA ☎ 480 2900; Carib Aviation ☎ 481 2400; Caribbean Star ☎ 480 2591; Continental ☎ 462-5355; LIAT ☎ 480 5600; Virgin ☎ 560 2079.

Airport departure tax For international flights the departure tax is presently US$20 (EC$50), payable at the airport when you leave.

Ambulance Emergency ☎ 911 or 999, otherwise ☎ 462 0251.

American Express Going Places Travel, corner of Long and Thames streets ☎ 481 2700, Mon–Thurs 8.30am–4.30pm, Fri 8.30am–5pm.

Banks St John's: Antigua Commercial Bank, St Mary's St at Thames St (Mon–Thurs 8am–2pm, Fri 8am–4pm); Bank of Antigua, Thames St at High St (Mon–Thurs 8am–3pm, Fri 8am–4pm, Sat 8am–12pm); First Caribbean International Bank, corner of High and Market streets (Mon–Thurs 8am–2pm, Fri 8am–4pm); ABIB, Woods Centre (Mon–Thurs 9am–3pm, Fri 9am–4pm, Sat 9am–1pm). Nelson's Dockyard: Bank of Antigua (just inside entrance of dockyard; Mon–Thurs 8am–3pm, Fri 8am–4pm, Sat 8am–12pm)

Dentists Antigua Barbuda Dental Group, Newgate St ☎ 460 3368; Dr Maxwell Francis, Cross St at Newgate St ☎ 462 0058; Dr Sengupta, Woods Centre ☎ 462 9312.

Embassies British High Commission, 11 Old Parham, St John's ☎ 462 0008; US Consular Agent (Rebecca Simon) ☎ 463 6531. There is no Australian, Canadian, Irish, or New Zealand embassy or commission in Antigua.

Film and photography equipment Island Photo (☎ 462 1567, Mon–Sat 8.30am–4.30pm), at the corner of Redcliffe and Market streets, sells film and does one-hour photo development; The Camera Shop, on Heritage Quay, offers the same service and has various camera accessories at duty-free prices.

Fire department ☎ 462 0044 or in the case of an emergency ☎ 911 or 999.

Hospitals St John's has the 225-bed public Holberton Hospital (☎ 462 0251). Smaller health centres and clinics are distributed around the island including the Adelin Medical Centre on Fort Rd (☎ 462 0866).

Internet access There is an Internet café beside the customs office in Nelson's Dockyard and another at the Yacht Club Marina on Falmouth Harbour; access is also available in St John's across from the *City View Hotel* and at the base of Heritage Quay by the cruise ship dock. Expect to pay EC$7 for 30 minutes.

Laundry Jolly Harbour: Burton's ☎ 462 7754; Falmouth Harbour: Sam & Dave's ☎ 460 1266; Nelson's Dockyard: near the dockyard café, no phone, daily 8am–5.30pm; St John's: Burton's, Independence Drive ☎ 462 4268.

Pharmacies Full service pharmacies in St John's: Benjamin's, Redcliffe St near Market St ☎ 462 0733 (Mon–Sat 8am–6pm), and Woods, Woods Centre ☎ 462 9287 (Mon–Sat 9am–10pm, Sun 11am–6pm). Jolly Harbour: Sysco ☎ 462 5917 (Mon–Sat 9am–5.30pm, Sun 12pm–4pm).

Police The main police station is on Newgate St ☎ 462 0045. For emergencies call ☎ 462 0125 or ☎ 999 or 911.

Post office English Harbour: Mon–Fri 8.15am–4pm; St John's: bottom of Long St, Mon–Fri 8.15am–4pm; Woods

Fly Less – Stay Longer!

Rough Guides believes in the good that travel does, but we are deeply aware of the impact of fuel emissions on climate change. We recommend taking fewer trips and staying for longer. If you can avoid travelling by air, please use an alternative, especially for journeys of under 1000km/600miles. And always offset your travel at ⓦ www.roughguides.com/climatechange.

Centre, Mon–Thurs 8.30am–3.50pm, Fri 8.30am–4.50pm.

Supermarkets English Harbour: Dockside Supermarket, Yacht Club Marina, Mon–Sat 8am–7pm, Sun 9am–4pm; Falmouth: C.E. Bailey, opposite *Harbour View Apartments*, daily 8am–7pm; Jolly Harbour: Epicurean, daily 8am–8pm; St John's: Epicurean, Woods Centre, daily 8am–9pm.

Taxis West Bus Station Taxis ☎ 462 5190; Antigua Reliable ☎ 460 5353. Both of these companies offer 24-hour service.

Travel agents English Harbour: Going Places Travel at Nicholson's, on the approach to Nelson's Dockyard ☎ 481 2712 (Mon–Sat 9am–4pm); St John's: Going Places Travel, Long St at Thames St ☎ 481 2700 (Mon–Fri 8am–4pm, Sat 8am–noon).

Travel store

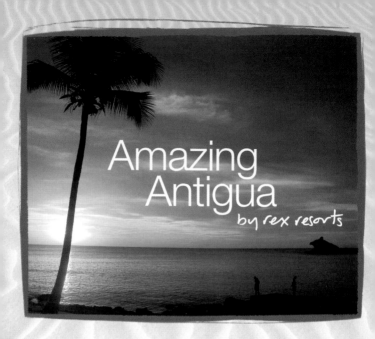

Chill|in
Paradise

Chillin out is easy at Jolly Beach
Resort Antigua... set in 40 acres of
tropical gardens, this all-inclusive
island paradise sits on one of the most
spectacular white-sand beaches in the
Caribbean. With 5 restaurants, 6 bars,
2 pools and our famous Caribbean
hospitality, we ensure your holiday
at Jolly Beach Resort will be an
unforgettable one.

**an exceptional
caribbean experience**

JOLLY
BEACH
RESORT
ANTIGUA

Free phone from UK 0800 804 8787
www.jollybeachresort.com

UK & Ireland
Britain
Devon & Cornwall
Dublin **D**
Edinburgh **D**
England
Ireland
The Lake District
London
London **D**
London Mini Guide
Scotland
Scottish Highlands & Islands
Wales

Europe
Algarve **D**
Amsterdam
Amsterdam **D**
Andalucía
Athens **D**
Austria
Baltic States
Barcelona
Barcelona **D**
Belgium & Luxembourg
Berlin
Brittany & Normandy
Bruges **D**
Brussels
Budapest
Bulgaria
Copenhagen
Corfu
Corsica
Costa Brava **D**
Crete
Croatia
Cyprus
Czech & Slovak Republics
Denmark
Dodecanese & East Aegean Islands
Dordogne & The Lot
Europe
Florence & Siena
Florence **D**
France
Germany

Gran Canaria **D**
Greece
Greek Islands
Hungary
Ibiza & Formentera **D**
Iceland
Ionian Islands
Italy
The Italian Lakes
Languedoc & Roussillon
Lanzarote & Fuerteventura **D**
Lisbon **D**
The Loire Valley
Madeira **D**
Madrid **D**
Mallorca **D**
Mallorca & Menorca
Malta & Gozo **D**
Menorca
Moscow
The Netherlands
Norway
Paris
Paris **D**
Paris Mini Guide
Poland
Portugal
Prague
Prague **D**
Provence & the Côte D'Azur
Pyrenees
Romania
Rome
Rome **D**
Sardinia
Scandinavia
Sicily
Slovenia
Spain
St Petersburg
Sweden
Switzerland
Tenerife & La Gomera **D**
Turkey
Tuscany & Umbria
Venice & The Veneto
Venice **D**
Vienna

Asia
Bali & Lombok
Bangkok
Beijing
Cambodia
China
Goa
Hong Kong & Macau
Hong Kong & Macau **D**
India
Indonesia
Japan
Laos
Malaysia, Singapore & Brunei
Nepal
The Philippines
Singapore
Singapore **D**
South India
Southeast Asia
Sri Lanka
Taiwan
Thailand
Thailand's Beaches & Islands
Tokyo
Vietnam

Australasia
Australia
Melbourne
New Zealand
Sydney

North America
Alaska
Baja California
Boston
California
Canada
Chicago
Colorado
Florida
The Grand Canyon
Hawaii
Las Vegas **D**
Los Angeles
Maui **D**
Miami & South Florida
Montréal
New England
New Orleans **D**
New York City

New York City **D**
New York City Mini Guide
Orlando & Walt Disney World® **D**
Pacific Northwest
San Francisco
San Francisco **D**
Seattle
Southwest USA
Toronto
USA
Vancouver
Washington DC
Washington DC **D**
Yellowstone & The Grand Tetons
Yosemite

Caribbean & Latin America
Antigua & Barbuda **D**
Argentina
Bahamas
Barbados **D**
Belize
Bolivia
Brazil
Cancún & Cozumel **D**
Caribbean
Central America
Chile
Costa Rica
Cuba
Dominican Republic
Dominican Republic **D**
Ecuador
Guatemala
Jamaica
Mexico
Peru
St Lucia **D**
South America
Trinidad & Tobago
Yúcatan

Africa & Middle East
Cape Town & the Garden Route
Dubai **D**

Available from all good bookstores   D: Rough Guide DIRECTIONS

Egypt
Gambia
Jordan
Kenya
Marrakesh **D**
Morocco
South Africa,
 Lesotho &
 Swaziland
Syria
Tanzania
Tunisia
West Africa
Zanzibar

Travel Specials
First-Time Africa
First-Time
 Around the
 World
First-Time Asia
First-Time
 Europe
First-Time Latin
 America
Travel Health
Travel Online
Travel Survival
Walks in London
 & SE England
Women Travel
World Party

Maps
Algarve
Amsterdam
Andalucia
 & Costa del Sol
Argentina
Athens
Australia
Barcelona
Berlin
Boston &
 Cambridge
Brittany
Brussels
California
Chicago
Chile
Corsica
Costa Rica
 & Panama
Crete
Croatia
Cuba
Cyprus
Czech Republic
Dominican
 Republic

Dubai & UAE
Dublin
Egypt
Florence & Siena
Florida
France
Frankfurt
Germany
Greece
Guatemala &
 Belize
Iceland
India
Ireland
Italy
Kenya &
 Northern
 Tanzania
Lisbon
London
Los Angeles
Madrid
Malaysia
Mallorca
Marrakesh
Mexico
Miami & Key
 West
Morocco
New England
New York City
New Zealand
Northern Spain
Paris
Peru
Portugal
Prague
Pyrenees &
 Andorra
Rome
San Francisco
Sicily
South Africa
South India
Spain & Portugal
Sri Lanka
Tenerife
Thailand
Toronto
Trinidad &
 Tobago
Tunisia
Turkey
Tuscany
Venice
Vietnam, Laos
 & Cambodia
Washington DC
Yucatán

Peninsula

**Dictionary
Phrasebooks**
Croatian
Czech
Dutch
Egyptian Arabic
French
German
Greek
Hindi & Urdu
Italian
Japanese
Latin American
 Spanish
Mandarin
 Chinese
Mexican Spanish
Polish
Portuguese
Russian
Spanish
Swahili
Thai
Turkish
Vietnamese

Computers
Blogging
eBay
iPods, iTunes
 & music online
The Internet
Macs & OS X
MySpace
PCs and Windows
PlayStation
 Portable
Website Directory

Film & TV
American
 Independent
 Film
British Cult
 Comedy
Chick Flicks
Comedy Movies
Cult Movies
Film Musicals
Film Noir
Gangster Movies
Horror Movies
Kids' Movies
Sci-Fi Movies
Westerns

Lifestyle
Babies

Ethical Living
Pregnancy
 & Birth

Music Guides
The Beatles
Blues
Bob Dylan
Book of Playlists
Classical Music
Elvis
Frank Sinatra
Heavy Metal
Hip-Hop
Jazz
Opera
Pink Floyd
Punk
Reggae
Rock
The Rolling
 Stones
Soul and R&B
World Music
 (2 vols)

Popular Culture
Books for
 Teenagers
Children's Books,
 5-11
Conspiracy
 Theories
Crime Fiction
Cult Fiction
The Da Vinci
 Code
Lord of the Rings
Shakespeare
Superheroes
Unexplained
 Phenomena

Science
The Brain
Climate Change
The Earth
Genes & Cloning
The Universe
Weather

For more information go to www.roughguides.com

ROUGH
GUIDES

- **Read** Rough Guides' trusted travel info

- **Access** exclusive articles from Rough Guides authors

- **Update** yourself on new books, maps, CDs and other products

- **Enter** our competitions and win travel prizes

- **Share** ideas, journals, photos & travel advice with other users

- **Earn** points every time you contribute to the Rough Guide
  community and get rewards

BROADEN YOUR HORIZONS

small print & Index

A Rough Guide to Rough Guides

In 1981, Mark Ellingham, a recent graduate in English from Bristol University, was travelling in Greece on a tiny budget and couldn't find the right guidebook. With a group of friends he wrote his own guide, combining a contemporary, journalistic style with a practical approach to travellers' needs. That first Rough Guide was a student scheme that became a publishing phenomenon. Today, Rough Guides include recommendations from shoestring to luxury and cover hundreds of destinations around the globe, including almost every country in the Americas and Europe, more than half of Africa and most of Asia and Australasia. Millions of readers relish Rough Guides' wit and inquisitiveness as much as their enthusiastic, critical approach and value-for-money ethos. The guides' ever-growing team of authors and photographers is spread all over the world.

In the early 1990s, Rough Guides branched out of travel, with the publication of Rough Guides to World Music, Classical Music and the Internet. All three have become benchmark titles in their fields, spearheading the publication of a range of more than 350 titles under the Rough Guide name, including phrasebooks, waterproof maps, music guides from Opera to Heavy Metal, reference works as diverse as Conspiracy Theories and Shakespeare, and popular culture books from iPods to Poker. Rough Guides also produce a series of more than 120 World Music CDs in partnership with World Music Network.

Visit www.roughguides.com to see our latest publications.

Rough Guide travel images are available for commercial licensing at www.roughguidespictures.com

Publishing information

This second edition published April 2007 by
Rough Guides Ltd, 80 Strand, London WC2R 0RL.
345 Hudson St, 4th Floor, New York, NY 10014, USA.

Distributed by the Penguin Group
Penguin Books Ltd, 80 Strand, London WC2R 0RL
Penguin Group (USA), 375 Hudson Street, NY
10014, USA
14 Local Shopping Centre, Panchsheel Park, New
Delhi 110017, India
Penguin Group (Australia), 250 Camberwell Road,
Camberwell, Victoria 3124, Australia
Penguin Group (Canada), 10 Alcorn Avenue,
Toronto, ON M4V 1E4, Canada
Penguin Group (NZ), 67 Apollo Drive, Mairangi Bay,
Auckland 1310, New Zealand
Typeset in Bembo and Helvetica to an original
design by Henry Iles.

Cover concept by Peter Dyer.

Printed and bound in China

144pp includes index

A catalogue record for this book is available from
the British Library

ISBN 10: 1-84353-755-9

ISBN 13: 978-1-84353-755-7

The publishers and authors have done their best to
ensure the accuracy and currency of all the information in Antigua & Barbuda DIRECTIONS, however,
they can accept no responsibility for any loss, injury,
or inconvenience sustained by any traveller as a
result of information or advice contained in the guide.

1   3   5   7   9   8   6   4   2

Help us update

We've gone to a lot of effort to ensure that the second edition of Antigua & Barbuda DIRECTIONS is accurate and up-to-date. However, things change – places get "discovered", opening hours are notoriously fickle, restaurants and rooms raise prices or lower standards. If you feel we've got it wrong or left something out, we'd like to know, and if you can remember the address, the price, the phone number, so much the better.

We'll credit all contributions, and send a copy of the next edition (or any other DIRECTIONS guide or Rough Guide if you prefer) for the best letters. Everyone who writes to us and isn't already a subscriber will receive a copy of our full-colour thrice-yearly newsletter. Please mark letters: "Antigua & Barbuda DIRECTIONS Update" and send to: Rough Guides, 80 Strand, London WC2R 0RL, or Rough Guides, 4th Floor, 345 Hudson St, New York, NY 10014. Or send an email to mail@roughguides.com

Have your questions answered and tell others about your trip at www.roughguides.atinfopop.com

Rough Guide credits

Text editor: AnneLise Sorensen
Layout: Anita Singh
Photography: Christopher P. Hamilton,
Ian Cumming
Cartography: Jasbir Sandhu, Maxine Repath,
Katie Lloyd-Jones

Picture editor: Mark Thomas
Proofreader: David Paul
Production: Aimee Hampson
Design: Henry Iles
Cover design: Chloë Roberts

SMALL PRINT

The author

Adam Vaitilingam is the author of many books on the Caribbean. He lives in Bristol.

Acknowledgements

Chris Hamilton thanks his fiancée Rebecca, his parents and his friends old and new in Antigua and Barbuda. He would like to dedicate his efforts to the memory of Desmond Nicholson, who was a true friend to the people and visitors of Antigua and Barbuda.

The editor would like to thank Chris Hamilton, Anita Singh, Karobi Gogoi, Maxine Repath, Katie Lloyd-Jones, Mark Thomas, David Paul and Andrew Rosenberg.

Photo credits

All images © Rough Guides except the following:

Front image: Coco Point beach © Alamy
Back image: St John's © Getty
p.10 Sailing off Antigua © Dave G. Houser/Corbis
p.11 Steel band at Carnival © Ian Cumming/Axiom

Index

Maps are marked in colour

a

accommodation (by area)
  Atlantic coast 66
  Barbuda 108
  Falmouth and English
    Harbour 83
  northwest coast 55
  St John's 45
  west coast 95
accommodation (by name) 118
  Admiral's Inn 83
  Anchorage Inn 55
  Antigua Village 55
  Antigua Yacht Club Marina
    Resort 83
  Barrymore Beach Club 55
  Beach House, The 108
  Blue Waters 66
  Carlisle Bay 95
  Carriage House, The 108
  Catamaran Hotel 83
  Chez Pascal 95
  City View Hotel 45
  Coco Point 108
  Cocobay Resort 95
  Coconut Beach Club 96
  Cocos 96
  Copper and Lumber Store 84
  Curtain Bluff 96
  Dian Bay Resort and Spa 67
  Dickenson Bay Cottages 55
  Galleon Beach 84
  Galley Bay 97
  Grand Royal Antiguan 96
  Harbour View Apartments 84
  Harmony Hall 67
  Hawksbill Beach 97
  Heritage Hotel 45
  Inn at English Harbour 84
  Island Chalet 108
  Joe Mike's Hotel 45
  Jolly Beach Resort 97
  Jolly Harbour Villas 97
  K Club 108
  Long Bay Hotel 67
  Lord Nelson Beach Hotel 67
  Marina Bay Hotel 55
  Mel's Guest House 45
  Nedd's Guesthouse 109
  North Beach 109
  Occidental Grand Pineapple
    Beach 68
  Ocean Inn 84
  Palm Bay Beach Club 68
  Pineapple House 84
  Rex Blue Heron 97
  Rex Halcyon Cove 56
  St James Club 85
  Sandals Antigua 56

  Siboney Beach Club 56
  Sunsail Club Colonna 68
  Tank Bay House Rooms 85
  Trade Winds Hotel 57
Admiral's Inn 76
airlines 129
airport departure tax 129
all-inclusives 118
aloe vera 120
Ambrose, Curtly 83
ambulance 129
American Express 129
Antigua Tourist Office 115
Antigua Yacht Club Marina 75
Antiguan food 20, 119
arrival 113
Atlantic coast, the 60–69
Atlantic coast 61

b

banks 117, 129
Barbuda 30, 101–110
Barbuda 102
  accommodation 108
  bars 109
  beaches 104
  boats 105
  caves 31
  Codrington 31, 101
  Codrington Lagoon 102
  flights 105
  Frigate bird sanctuary 31, 103
  getting there 105
  Highlands House 103
  Indian Caves 104
  Martello Tower 31
  Palm Beach 30
  Palmetto Point 30
  Redonda 106
  restaurants 109
  River Fort 106
  shipwrecks 107
  shops 110
  Spanish Point 30, 106
  taxis 105
bars (by area)
  Atlantic coast 69
  Barbuda 109
  Falmouth and English
    Harbour 85
  northwest coast 57
  St John's 46
  west coast 98
bars (by name)
  After Hours Bar 46
  Bumpkins 85
  C&C Wine Bar 46

  Candyland 58
  Castaways 98
  Chill Out Bar 69
  Dogwatch Tavern 98
  Gallery Bar and Grill 87
  Green Door Tavern 109
  Life 87
  Lime, The 110
  OJ's Beach Bar 99
  Shamarooney's Pub 48
  Sticky Wicket, The 70
  Tamarind Bar and
    Restaurant 70
  Turner's Beach Bar & Grill 100
beaches 12
  Carlisle Bay 92
  Coco Beach 93
  Darkwood Beach 13, 93
  Devil's Bridge 65
  Dickenson Bay 12, 18, 52, 121
  Fort Bay 51
  Galleon Beach 80
  Green Island 12, 66
  Half Moon Bay 13, 66
  Hawksbill Bay 94
  Jabberwock Beach 19, 62
  Long Bay 65
  Palm Beach 30, 104
  Palmetto Point 30, 105
  Pigeon Beach 13, 78
  Rendezvous Bay 13, 71, 72
  Runaway Bay 52
  Turner's Beach 93
  Two Foot Bay 105
  White Bay 105
beer 20, 119
Betty's Hope 10, 22, 64
bicycling 114, 125
birdwatching 54
boat operators 123
boats 122
Boggy Peak 25, 92
Botanical Garden, Victoria
  Park 39
buses 113

c

Cape Shirley 81
car rental 114
Carlisle Bay 92
Carnival 11, 40
Carpenter Rock Trail 82
cars 73, 114
catamarans 122
caves 31, 104
cell phones 118
children, travelling with 127

Clarence House 79
climate 4
Coco Beach 93
Codrington 31, 101
Codrington 104
Codrington Lagoon 102
colonial forts 16
communication 117
costs 116
credit cards 116
cricket 42, 62, 126
crime 127
cruise operators 123
currency 116
cycling 114, 125

d

Darkwood Beach 13, 93
Deep Bay 94
dentists 129
departure tax 129
Devil's Bridge 29, 65
Dickenson Bay 12, 10, 52
diving 121
Dockyard Museum 77
Dow's Hill Fort 16, 81
drinking 20, 119

e

electrical current 118
embassies 129
English Harbour 75
events 128

f

Falmouth and English Harbour 24, 71–89
Falmouth and English Harbour area 72
Falmouth and English Harbour 74
festivals 128
Fig Tree Drive 28, 90
film 129
fire department 129
fishing 124
Fitches Creek Bay 63
Five Islands peninsula 94
flights 113
food 20, 119
Fort Barrington 17, 94
Fort Bay 51
Fort Berkeley 17, 77
Fort Cuyler 78
Fort James 16, 51

Fort Shirley 80
Frigate bird sanctuary 31
fruit 21, 119

g

Galleon Beach 80
galleries 22
golf 125
Great Fort George 17, 72
Green Castle Hill 94
Green Island 12, 66

h

Half Moon Bay 13, 66
Harmony Hall 23, 65
Hawksbill Bay 94
Hawksbill Rock 29
Heritage Quay 38
hiking 24, 126
Hodges Bay 60
holidays, public 128
horseback riding 125
hospitals 129
hotels see accommodation

i

Independence Avenue 43
Indian Caves 104
Indian Creek 24, 82
international calls 117
Internet access 129

j

Jabberwock Reach 10, 62
Jolly Harbour 93

k

kayaking 18
King's Casino 39
kiteboarding 19, 62

l

laundry 129
Liberta 83
Long Bay 65
Lookout, The 82

m

Mamora Bay 82
Manchineel trees 120
maps 115
Martello tower 31
McKinnon's Salt Pond 54
Middle Ground 25, 78
military cemetery 81
minibuses 113
mobile phones 118
money 116
motorbikes 114
museums 22

n

Nanton, Pat 126
National Museum 22, 41
Nelson's Dockyard 11, 75
Nelson's Dockyard Museum 23, 75
Nelson's Dockyard officers' quarters 77
newspapers 118
Nick Maley's Island Arts Gallery 23
nightlife (by area)
    Falmouth and English Harbour 89
    northwest coast 59
    St John's 49
    west coast 100
nightlife (by name) 26
    18 Karat 49
    Abracadabra 27, 88
    Beach, The 59
    Coast, The 50
    Conor's Sports Bar 59
    Deluxe Cinema 50
    Dry Dock, The 89
    Grand Princess Casino 26, 100
    Grand Royal Antiguan 100
    Jolly Harbour entertainment complex 26
    Last Lemming, The 89
    Life 27, 89
    Liquid Nightclub 26, 100
    Lookout, The 27, 89
    Rasta Shack, The 27, 89
    Rush Nightclub 59
    Steely Bar 100
northwest coast, the 51–59
northwest coast 53

o

Old Road 92
outdoor activities 18, 24, 121

p

Palm Beach 30, 104
Palmetto Point 30, 105
Paradise Reef 121
Parham Harbour 63
passport 113
pepperpot stew 21
personal safety 127
pharmacies 129
Pigeon Beach 13, 78
Pillars of Hercules 29, 80
police 129
post office 129
postal service 117
Prickly Pear Island 62, 121
public holidays 128
public market 21, 44

r

radio 118
Rec, The 39
Redcliffe Quay 38
Redonda 106
Rendezvous Bay 13, 24, 71
Rendezvous Trail 92
restaurants (by area) 69
  Atlantic coast 69
  Barbuda 108
  Falmouth and English
    Harbour 85
  northwest coast 57
  St John's 46
  west coast 98
restaurants (by name) 14
  Abracadabra 85
  Admiral's Inn 85
  Bay House 57
  Beach, The 57
  Beach House, The 69, 109
  Big Banana – Pizzas in
    Paradise 46
  Bumpkins 85
  Café Napoleon 46
  Calabash 85
  Caribbean Taste 86
  Castaways 98
  Catherine's Café 86
  Chez Pascal 15, 98
  Cloggy's 86
  Coconut Grove 14, 58
  Cocos 98
  Commissioner Grill 47
  Cove, The 69
  Dockyard Bakery 86
  Dogwatch Tavern 98
  East 98
  Famous Mauro's 86
  Gallery Bar and Grill 87
  George 47
  Grace Before Meals 87

Harmony Hall 15, 69
Hemingway's 47
Home 14, 47
Indigo on the Beach 99
Jackee's Kwik Stop 87
Joe Mike's 47
Last Lemming, The 87
Le Bistro 69
Le Cap Horn 87
Life 87
Lookout, The 87
Mad Mongoose, The 87
Mainbrace, The 88
Mama Lolly's Vegetarian
  Café 47
Mama's Pasta 70
Mellini's Ristorante and
  Pizzeria 99
Millers by the Sea 58
OJ's Beach Bar 99
Palm Tree 110
Papa Zouk 15, 47
Pari's Pizza 58
Park Terrace Restaurant 110
Peter's BBQ Steakhouse 99
Putters 58
Roti King 48
Russell's 58
Sheer 15, 99
Steely Bar 99
Sticky Wicket, The 70
Tamarind Bar and
  Restaurant 70
Trappas 88
Turner's Beach Bar & Grill 100
Wa'Omoni's Best 110
Warri Pier 59
Richards, Viv 42, 126
River Fort 106
Roberts, Andy 42
rum 21, 119
Runaway Bay 52

s

safety 120
sailing 19, 123
Sailing Week 10, 77
St George's Parish Church
  63
St John's 35–49
St John's 36–37
  accommodation 45
  bars 46
  buses 38
  Carnival 40
  entertainment 49
  Heritage Quay 38
  Independence Avenue 43
  information 38
  King's Casino 39
  National Museum 41
  nightlife 49
  public market 44
  Rec, The 39

Redcliffe Quay 38
  restaurants 46
  Cathedral 42
  shopping 49
  taxis 38
  V.C. Bird statue 45
  Victoria Park Botanical
    Garden 39
St Peter's Anglican Church
  63
St Stephen's Anglican
  Church 63
sea urchins 120
Seatons 63
Shiell, Matthew 107
shipwrecks 107
Shirley Heights 11, 25, 79
Shirley Heights Lookout 29
shops
  Art Café 110
  Authentic Barbudan
    Souvenirs 110
  British-American Mall 49
  Food Emporium
    Supermarket 49
  Island Arts Gallery 49
  National Museum Gift
    Shop 49
  The Map & Book Shop 49
  Woods Centre 49
  Woods Gallery 49
snorkelling 106, 121
Soldier Point 66
Spanish Point 30, 106
sports 121
squash 125
Stanford Cricket Ground 62
Sunsail Club Colonna 19
supermarkets 130
Swetes 83

t

taxis 114, 130
telephone calls 117
tennis 125
tourist information 115
tours 114
transport 113
travel agents 130
travellers' cheques 116
Turner's Beach 93
Two Foot Bay 105

v

V.C. Bird statue 45
vegetables 21, 119
Victoria Park Botanical
  Garden 39
visas 113

Wadadli beer 20
Wadadli Cats 19
Wallings Woodlands 25
watersports 18, 121

weather 4
west coast, the 90–100
west coast 91
White Bay 105
Willoughby Bay 82
windsurfing 18, 124
wiring money 117

yachting charters 124